Breed Standard for the German Shepherd Dog

Body
Length, measured from point of breast bone to rear edge of pelvis, exceeding height at withers.

General Appearance
Slightly long in comparison to height; of powerful, well muscled build with weather-resistant coat.

Croup
Long, gently curving downwards to tail without disrupting flowing topline.

Hindquarters
Overall strong, broad and well muscled, enabling effortless forward propulsion of whole body. Any tendency towards over-angulation of hindquarters reduces firmness and endurance.

Tail
Bushy-haired, reaches at least to hock—ideal length reaching to middle of metatarsus. At rest tail hangs in slight sabre-like curve; when moving raised and curve increased, ideally never above level of back.

Colour
Black or black saddle with tan, or gold to light grey markings. All black, all grey, with lighter or brown markings referred to as Sables.

Coat
Outer coat consisting of straight, hard, close-lying hair as dense as possible; thick undercoat.

Photo credits:

Norvia Behling
Carolina Biological Supply
Liza Clancy
David Dalton
Marcus Degen
Fleabusters, Rx for Fleas
Isabelle Francais
Detlof Handschack
James E. Hayden, RBP
James Hayden-Yoav
Carol Ann Johnson
Alice van Kempen

Klaar
Dwight R. Kuhn
Dr. Dennis Kunkel
Alice Pantfoeder
Antonio Phillipe
Phototake
Meg Purnell-Carpenter
Jean Claude Revy
M. A. Stevenson, DVM
Nikki Sussman
Christina Urban
C. James Webb

Guide dogs pictured are trained at The Seeing Eye®, Morristown, NJ, USA.

DISTRIBUTED BY: **INTERPET**
PUBLISHING

Vincent Lane, Dorking, Surrey RH4 3YX England

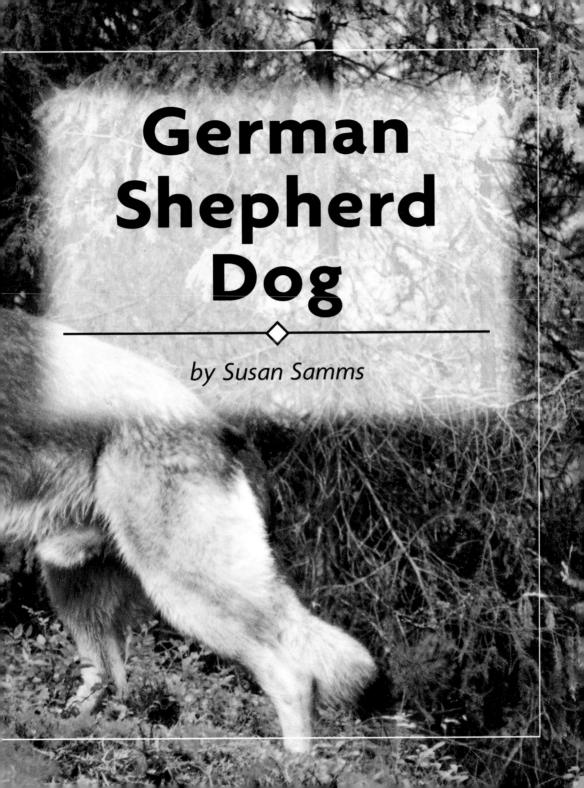

German Shepherd Dog

by Susan Samms

Table of Contents

8 Ancestry of the German Shepherd Dog

14 Why the German Shepherd Dog?

24 Breed Standard for the German Shepherd Dog

32 Your German Shepherd Puppy

52 Everyday Care of Your German Shepherd Dog

ISBN 13: 978 0 966859 20 1
ISBN 10: 0 966859 20 0

Housebreaking and Training
Your German Shepherd Dog **66**
by Charlotte Schwartz

Health Care of
German Shepherd Dogs **90**

When Your
German Shepherd Dog Gets Old **118**

Showing Your
German Shepherd Dog **124**

Understanding Your
Dog's Behaviour **136**

Glossary **153**   Index **156**

The German Shepherd is at home outdoors in the field.

Ancestry of the German Shepherd Dog

'...as hounds and greyhounds,
mongrels, spaniels, curs
Shoughs, water-rugs, and
demi-wolves are clept
All by the name of dogs.
The valued file
Distinguishes the swift,
the slow, the subtle
The housekeeper, the hunter,
every one
According to the gift which
bounteous nature
Hath in him closed, whereby
he does receive
Particular addition from the bill
That writes them all alike...'
—Macbeth

HISTORY AND ORIGINAL PURPOSE IN GERMANY

The particular qualifications that set the German Shepherd Dog apart from the general catalogue that lists all breeds are numerous and evident from the first moment in the history of the animal.

Considerations of companionship and domination aside, the first domesticated canines were utilised for practical and essential purposes such as the guarding and control of livestock. From the crude animals that helped early shepherds with their flocks, evolved light-gaited, weather-impervious, dependable animals, commonly categorised as sheepdogs.

German Shepherd Dogs are still used for sheep-herding.

9

In 1891 a group of German admirers of this rugged, unrefined dog formed the Phylax Society, named after the Greek word *phylaxis,* which means to watch over or guard. The purpose of this organisation was to standardise the varied collection of sheep-herding dogs into a breed of native German dog with a fixed appearance and character.

The Phylax Society lasted until only 1894, but its purpose and vision was continued in the person of one man, Max Emil Friedrich von Stephanitz, considered by many to be the single greatest force in the establishment of the German Shepherd Dog as a specific breed.

The originator of the breed was discovered by von Stephanitz on April 3, 1899, when he and another sheepdog enthusiast were attending an exhibition of these herding dogs. The dog they encountered was agile, powerful, alert and strongly adapted to its utilitarian purpose. To von Stephanitz, this animal seemed to be the perfect embodiment of the worker and guardian ideal that he held for this type of dog. The overt intelligence and desire to serve apparent in the dog's temperament belied its wild, wolfish appearance. Von Stephanitz bought the animal on the spot. Its original name, Hektor von Linksrhein, was changed to Horand von Grafrath and it was registered as German Shepherd Dog, S.Z. 1, the

In 1891 the development of the German Shepherd began. Its objective was to produce a German dog with a standard appearance and behaviour.

PHOTO BY CHRISTINA URBAN

Because the well-trained German Shepherd Dog is so eager to please its master (or mistress), it has been utilised in a variety of roles.

first entry in von Stephanitz's new organisation, Verein für Deutsche Schäferhunde. This is the beginning of the national German dog club known as the S.V., the largest individual breed club in the world.

Horand proved to be an able stud and the traits that von Stephanitz prized at first meeting were passed on to succeeding dogs and strengthened by this early breeder's careful policies of close inbreeding, called linebreeding, a practice which seeks to emphasise and strengthen desirable characteristics through determined genetic management in the kennel and farm.

Always foremost in von Stephanitz's mind was the working, practical ideal of the breed. From the beginning, form in the German Shepherd Dog was not intended to deviate from function. Von Stephanitz foresaw an early threat to the breed's validity as working animals when human society passed from a largely agricultural and agrarian basis to an industrialised economy. As a first step, he persuaded the German government to accept the breed for police work. This was the beginning of the breed's association with law enforcement and military use. Soon the animal's qualities of intelligence, reliability and hardiness, the central aspects of its character and existence in history, secured its use in many important roles, most noble of which is the dog's role as a guide for the blind.

Despite the surges and declines in the breed's popularity throughout history, today the German Shepherd is one of the most respected breeds in the world.

THE BREED OUTSIDE OF GERMANY

The close attachment of the German Shepherd Dog to human kind is revealed in its very name, which identifies a human occupation. This strong association and identification has both rewarded and plagued the breed and this is clearly revealed in the animal's interesting American history.

The first German Shepherd Dogs were introduced to America around 1906 by wealthy collectors and breeders. The breed soon won influential admirers, but the advent of World War I put an abrupt halt to its growing popularity because of the dog's close identification with its country of origin.

The breed's popularity declined for a second time as anti-German feeling resurged in the United States and Allied Europe during World War II. So deep was the prejudice against the dog's national origin, that its supporters attempted, with little success, to disguise the breed by calling it the Alsatian Wolf Dog. To this day, the dog is often referred to as an 'Alsatian,' a name which associates it with a less problematical region of Europe.

Again it was the breed's close association with humankind and not its intrinsic character that brought about decline. And again it was the hard work and noble effort of these dogs in various military and life-saving capacities that renewed admiration and avid acceptance. So intense became the demand for this breed that unscrupulous and uncontrolled breeding led to many medical and behavioural problems, most notably hip

DID YOU KNOW?

It was not until after the war that the breed recaptured American favour, based this time upon its time-old qualities of service and intelligence. Many American soldiers returned from Europe with stories of the courage and reliability of the dogs that they had seen in military and Red Cross uses. Many also returned with the dogs themselves. This growing popularity was accelerated by two famous silent film heroes, who happened to be German Shepherd Dogs, Rin Tin Tin and Strongheart.

The original Rin Tin Tin was brought to the United States by a returned soldier. The dog lived for only thirteen years but others of the breed carried forward the name and role. Strongheart, equally popular at the time but less known today, was a fully trained police dog imported to America for work in the film industry.

dysplasia, which continue to plague the breed today.

Overbreeding also led to the fear biters and other neurotic specimens which threaten the reputation of this normally noble and kind dog.

During the 1960s, veterinary surgeons and protectors of the breed, most prominently the German Shepherd Dog Club of America and the German S.V., joined together to control these problems and to safeguard this breed of guardians.

Today there is a radiological method of determining hip dysplasia in individual dogs and certifying those free of it as dogs of breeding quality.

The American club has affixed a Register of Merit, or ROM, title to dogs whose offspring prove healthy and worthy of show. The S.V. has created Class I (dogs with no fault) and Class II (dogs with minor faults) rankings to underscore and protect the ideals of physical and mental soundness that were established by the architects of the breed.

Reputable breeders have followed suit to ensure the health and popularity of the breed. They not only scrutinise the backgrounds of sires and dams but also interrogate buyers about how they intend to raise and use their puppies.

The modern German Shepherd Dog has weathered a difficult and varied history, with the features that set it aside and above other breeds intact and zealously protected. It is fitting that the qualities of nobility and protection that brought these canine and human companions first together should continue to characterise their association.

The German Shepherd's character is evident in his noble expression.

For the past 100 years, the German Shepherd Dog has slowly evolved into one of the most desirable breeds. Puppies from properly bred, healthy parents are avidly sought after.

Why the German Shepherd Dog?

CHARACTERISTICS OF THE BREED

Those who are considering sharing a significant portion of their lives with a German Shepherd Dog will do well to discount the associations, good or bad, that have become attached to the dog throughout its intricate history and to concentrate upon the qualities and characteristics that first attracted von Stephanitz to the animal. The primal and, in this case, ideal German Shepherd Dog was agile, powerful, rugged, steady, alert and intelligent. Above all the dog delighted in work and purpose. This dog's association with man was neither servile nor amusing, nor was the dog ever intended to be an object of beauty or cultiva-

THE SEEING EYE®, MORRISTOWN, NJ, USA.

German Shepherd Dog owners love their dogs so much they often have portraits and statuettes commissioned in the dogs' honour.

tion. The German Shepherd Dog began on a footing as equal to man as canine ever achieved.

Such nobility of purpose perhaps cannot be sustained in the ordinary households that will be home to the vast majority of German Shepherd Dogs but the ideal should neither be forgotten nor ignored. Expect that you and your German Shepherd Dog will on some intrinsic level be equal and your relationship will be well founded.

PHYSICAL CHARACTERISTICS

Puppies have floppy ears that stand by six or seven months. Some dogs have ears that never stand. Although taping most often can correct this

---

DID YOU KNOW?

Originally intended for herding, German Shepherd Dogs were medium-sized but as guarding and other uses became predominant, the breed became progressively larger. Today adult males are 61-66 centimetres (24-26 inches) at the withers and females are approximately two inches smaller. The normal weight range is 30-40 kgs (66-88 lbs). Adult physical characteristics are achieved by 10-18 months, but dogs will typically fill out until three years of age. Large size is not necessarily preferred and may, in some case, exacerbate the tendency to certain orthopaedic disorders.

The all-weather coat of the German Shepherd does not require much time from its owner. This handsome chap has a fairly short coat.

fault, these dogs should be considered poor choices for breeding.

Conventional depictions of the breed emphasise the black and tan colouring with saddleback markings but the German Shepherd Dog comes in a wide variety of colours such as black and red, black and cream, all black, all white, sable (with various colourations), black and silver, liver and blue. Breeders do not favour the white, liver or blue varieties.

Coats are double, with the outer coarser coat serving to resist water and exterior matter, and the inner soft dense undercoat working to retain body heat during cold seasons. The fur can range from short and coarse to long and soft. Long-coated dogs, however, are not eligible for showing in the breed ring.

German Shepherd Dogs will shed all year long with heavy shedding during the spring and fall. Grooming, however, is not difficult. Regular light brushing is all that is required. Bathing, when necessary, should employ a hypoallergenic shampoo.

German Shepherd Dogs are serious animals, even when they are puppies. They observe strangers carefully.

The main concern of every admirer of the German Shepherd Dog is character. The animal should be courageous, intelligent, playful and safe with children and strongly obedient and responsive to its owner. These elements of sound disposition and utility supersede any and all physical ideals.

PERSONALITY

Throughout history, in whatever capacity the German Shepherd has been used, one thing that has been constant is the bond that has developed between the dogs and their owners. Since the dogs have traditionally been used as service and working dogs, this bond was a necessity. The dogs had to be very obedient and very reliable to perform their given tasks. Since a major role of the German Shepherd has been that of a guard dog, the dogs also had to be very protective of their owners. These characteristics translate into a pet dog that is very intelligent, highly trainable, and extremely loyal. The pet German Shep-

---

DID YOU KNOW?

The behaviour and personality of your German Shepherd Dog will reflect your care and training more than any breed characteristics or indications. Remember that these dogs require a purposeful existence and plan your relationship around activities that serve this most basic and important need. All the good potential of the breed will necessarily follow.

herd watches over the entire family and seems to be able to sense if someone is in trouble or needs help. Likewise, the German Shepherd is a wonderful protector of children and of his owner's property.

Due to these protective instincts, the German Shepherd is naturally wary of strangers. This is not to say that he is not a friendly dog, but he chooses whom to befriend based on his owner's attitude. "Any friend of yours is a friend of mine!" the German Shepherd seems to say to his owner,

German Shepherd Dogs were originally bred to be sheepherders and thus are naturally active dogs.

but he fiercely trusts his owner's judgment. The dog will warm up to people that he becomes familiar with; he looks to his owner for clues about who is "okay" and who is not. Proper socialisation and introduction to people from an early age is necessary to help the German Shepherd become more accepting of the people he meets.

The German Shepherd is noble and proud—he has a lot going for him and he knows it! A wonderful combination of stamina, athleticism, intelligence, grace and beauty, he personifies the virtues of "man's best friend."

OWNER SUITABILITY

Because the German Shepherd Dog is so devoted to his owner, it is only natural that he should thrive best with an owner who can show him equal devotion. The German Shepherd basks in his owner's attention. It is not necessarily true that the only type of person suitable to own a German Shepherd is one who is home all day, but the owner who spends the day at work must plan on time with the dog upon his return home.

Exercise is also a consideration for the German Shepherd. Remember, these dogs were bred to work and to be active. The breeders' original focus was on function. Since the pet dog is not being used for his intended purpose, he must be active in other ways. A German Shepherd who lives at home with his owner cannot exercise himself; it is something that both dog and owner need to participate in. It is not fair to the dog, who has patiently waited for his owner to return from work, for the owner to come home and promptly park himself on the couch for the remainder of the evening. Exercise is essential for the German Shepherd's well being, both physically and mentally. It provides this athletic breed with much-needed activity, plus it helps him feel like he has a purpose.

A house with a securely fenced-in garden may be ideal for a German Shepherd owner, as the dog will have some freedom to run and play by himself. The dog should still be under the owner's supervision when off-lead, but at least the dog will not be totally dependent on his owner for exercise. This does not make up for time spent with his owner,

PHOTO BY CHRISTINA URBAN.

Zwinger von Muldental and his young friend keep watch over the garden.

but will at least give the dog some physical benefits. An owner who keeps a German Shepherd in a house without a garden or in an apartment must make the commitment to regular runs/walks/playtime with the dog.

The German Shepherd will fit into just about any family structure…adults, children, single people, etc. It is just necessary that the breed's characteristics are taken into consideration.

VERSATILITY AND AGILITY

Although your German Shepherd Dog may never be required to do more than provide companionship and love to you and your family, you may be proud to consider the many functions that the breed can be called upon to perform.

The instinct to serve, which is born in the animal, is the foundation of its functional versatility along with its physical and mental traits of strength, size, endurance and intelligence. It would be fair to say that the majority of all service dogs in the world are German Shepherd Dogs. The potential for specific service lies within each German Shepherd Dog but professional training is required to actualise it in almost every case.

As previously noted, the German Shepherd dog is an excellent herding

DID YOU KNOW?

German Shepherd Dogs have been used as military dogs since World War I. Their roles have been numerous. The dogs served as sentries, guards, mine detectors, rescuers of wounded soldiers and carriers of food and medicine.

Only the most instructable and obedient German Shepherd Dogs are selected for service dog training.

dog. This was its original function and remains a central factor in its modern versatility. The breed's endurance, its rough-coated imperviousness to weather, its sure-footed speed, responsiveness and deep-rooted instinct to protect anything small or weak make it an ideal herding choice.

It is only in Germany, however, that the German Shepherd Dog is a first choice among farmers and stock owners. In the United States and Great Britain, other native breeds, more traditional and therefore more attractive to some, like the Australian Shepherd and the Border Collie are predominantly seen.

German Shepherd Dogs were especially impressive as scout dogs, often able to detect the presence of an enemy at 250 metres away. Countless human lives were saved by these dogs but many of the animals were sacrificed in services like mine detection.

From these military uses developed the breed's important role as police dogs. In the pursuit and apprehension of criminals the dog has proven itself valuable

and rather more effective, certainly more humane, than guns. The dog's cool nerves and intelligence make it an excellent choice for crowd control. Its scenting ability makes it invaluable in search and rescue work, as well as bomb and drug detection.

The skills and abilities of these two functions are combined in Schutzhund, a training and competition programme that emphasises the elements of protection. Schutzhund means 'protection dog' in German. Schutzhund trials have existed since the early 1900s. They include tests for temperament, tracking and protection. Dogs are scored according to their performance in these areas and must exhibit complete obedience (despite distraction), confidence,

The ultimate praise is the German Shepherd Dog's use as a guide dog for the blind.

DID YOU KNOW?

In Schutzhund trials, dogs are rated by performance and can earn the titles of SchHI (beginner), SchHII (intermediate) and SchHIII (master). These titles can be appended to the dog's name and pedigree.

courage, scenting ability, determination and concentration in tracking.

The preceding roles have stressed obedience founded upon the breed's natural proclivities. The German Shepherd Dog is not a particularly aggressive dog. It is, however, very protective of its family and property. This is the basis of the alertness and protective instinct that have made it a staple in institutional use and an effective watchdog for the home and family.

The most noble and pride-provoking use of the German Shepherd Dog has been in the service of people with physical challenges. The German Shepherd Dog was the first dog used as a guide dog for blind individuals and later for deaf individuals. The dog's initial employment as guides for blind World War I veterans led to the creation of the Seeing Eye® Foundation in 1929. Today this dog's traits of composure, intelligence and responsibility, combined with all of its other excellent aspects, continue to make it the first choice in this role and all of the other roles designed to serve humankind.

HEALTH CONSIDERATIONS AND HEREDITARY DISEASES

Given the care that love and respect for the animal demand, the German Shepherd Dog is a tough and healthy breed. It has been frequently stressed here that the German Shepherd Dog was, from its earliest history, developed as a working animal and, therefore, frequent and, above all, purposeful activity is essential to its health. Without regular exercise and activity, the breed is foremost susceptible to rheumatism, the symptoms of which are similar to those in humans: swelling and stiffening of the affected joints and pain in movement. Because some of the symptoms of this condition

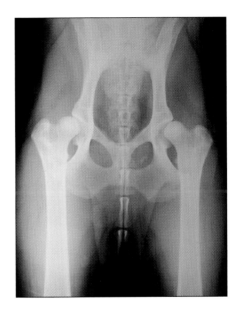

Barely perceptible hip dysplasia in a German Shepherd Dog must be treated as soon as possible.

are shared by the far more serious hip dysplasia, prompt professional attention is necessary when first displayed.

Skin problems are also frequent in the breed. Slow, constant scratching, as opposed to the short burst of scratching associated with fleas, is a sign of skin trouble. If observed early, the majority of these problems can be reduced quickly by veterinary care and diet.

Other diseases and conditions found in the German Shepherd Dogs are not exclusive to the breed but are shared by others of its various types. Because, for example, the German Shepherd Dog is a large breed, it is affected by osteochondritis dissecans, panosteitis, hypertrophic osteodystrophy and myasthenia gravis, all diseases of the bone.

Because of its shepherding nature, the German Shepherd Dog is prone to the eye conditions typical of this category of dog like collie eye, pannus, cataracts and retinal dysplasia.

Epilepsy is another condition that affects shepherding dogs. Blood conditions like von Willebrand's disease and hemophilia A, and heart problems such as patent or persistent ductus arteriosis and persistent right aortic arch, are problems that affect most canines and the German Shepherd Dog is not excluded.

No discussion of health concerning the German Shepherd Dog can end, however, without clear talk about hip dysplasia. German Shepherd Dogs have the highest percentage rate of HD of any

breed. The fact that it stands to reason that the most popular and excessively bred dog should most reveal this hereditary condition does nothing to ameliorate that fact.

Dysplastic dogs have incorrectly developed hip joints, prone to arthritis and wildly painful. These dogs are unable to work or even move easily and without discomfort. Breeders and veterinary surgeons continue to study this condition and guard against its occurrence but it is the responsibility of every prospective German Shepherd Dog owner to know that the parents and grandparents of their animal had hips rated good or better.

It is possible that part of the breed's predisposition to this condition may have been caused by the early developer's exaggeration of the powerful down-

Elbow dysplasia in a three-and-a-half-year-old male German Shepherd Dog.

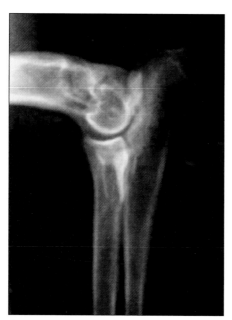 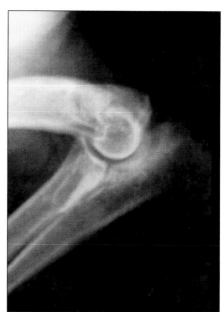

PHOTO COURTESY OF M. A. STEVENSON, DVM AND THE JOURNAL OF THE AMERICAN VETERINARY MEDICINE ASSOC.

Since the German Shepherd by nature is an active working dog, good health is an absolute necessity for all breed members. When selecting your German Shepherd puppy, do not shop for convenience and do not be thrifty. You deserve to have the best dog that your money can buy. A well-bred Shepherd from quality stock (lines that have been tested for hereditary problems for generations) is your best choice. Even though a Shepherd with only mild dysplasia can still lead a normal life, no one wants to see his best friend compromised in any fashion. The author strongly recommends that owners thoroughly investigate their puppies before purchase, so that your heart is not shattered by adopting a lovely dog with serious health problems.

ward curve of the animals' posture. If true, it is sad that the unassailable, largely unchanged character of this noble breed should be linked to this weakness, unknowingly fostered by its earliest and fondest architects.

Recently elbow dysplasia has become a concern and screening criteria have also been developed. Those genetic physical problems that the breed is heir to are considerations that are best countered by careful planning and care in the choice and selection of breeder and animal.

Although the list of congenital diseases to which German Shepherd Dogs are prone is somewhat daunting, most representatives of the breed are healthy indeed. Many Shepherds can live heartily past ten years of age, and some have been known to be exuberant teenagers.

Excelling in police work, the German Shepherd Dog has earned the highest accolades. Winning Police Dog Action for 1999 is Overhills Foggarty, bred by Meg Purnell-Carpenter and handled by WPC Leigh White.

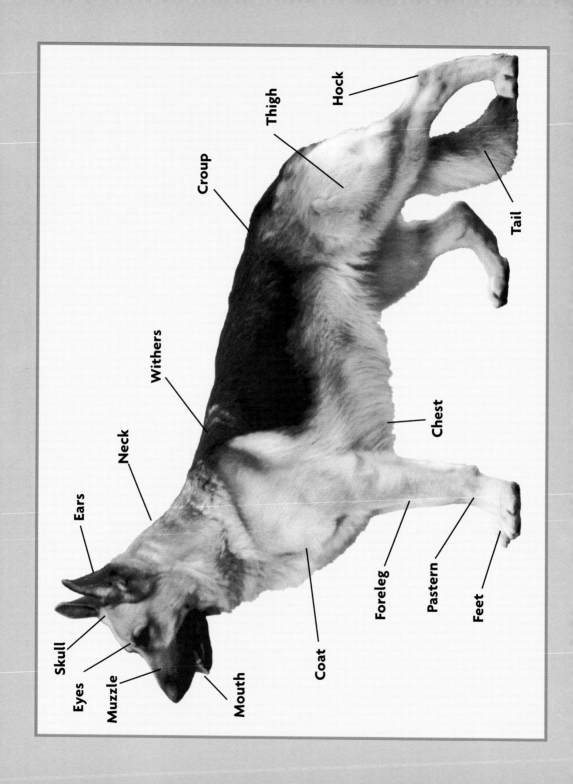

Breed Standard for the German Shepherd Dog

WHAT IS A BREED STANDARD?
A breed standard is a guide that breeders use to develop their breeding programs and judges use to evaluate dogs in a conformation show. It is a written blueprint of the ideal German Shepherd Dog. These standards are drawn up by the national breed club and then submitted to the national kennel club, the governing body of purebred dogs for a specific country, for acceptance. Despite differences in wording, the requirements are essentially the same from country to country, although there may be significant differences that should be noted. Breed standards are always subject to change, so it is a good idea to check with your national kennel club to keep up with the developments in your breed.

A typical German Shepherd Dog from American stock.

25

A head to tail description of the modern German Shepherd Dog will be revealed in the following breed standard.

THE KENNEL CLUB STANDARD
General Appearance: Slightly long in comparison to height; of powerful, well muscled build with weather-resistant coat. Relation between height, length, position and structure of fore and hindquarters (angulation) producing far-reaching, enduring gait. Clear definition of masculinity and femininity essential, and working ability never sacrificed for mere beauty.

Characteristics: Versatile working dog, balanced and free from exaggeration. Attentive, alert, resilient and tireless with keen scenting ability.

The German Shepherd's eyes should be almond-shaped and brown in colour. This black Shepherd, bred by the famous Overhills Kennels, has the desirable self-assured and alert expression.

Temperament: Steady of nerve, loyal, self-assured, courageous and tractable. Never nervous, over-aggressive or shy.

Head and Skull: Proportionate in size to body, never coarse, too fine or long. Clean cut; fairly broad between ears. Forehead slightly domed; little or no trace of central furrow. Cheeks forming softly rounded curve, never protruding. Skull from ears to bridge of nose tapering gradually and evenly, blending without too pronounced stop into a wedge-shaped powerful muzzle. Skull approximately 50 per cent of overall length of head. Width of skull corresponding approximately to length, in males slightly greater, in females slightly less. Muzzle strong, lips firm, clean and closing tightly. Top of muzzle straight, almost parallel to forehead. Short, blunt, weak, pointed, overlong muzzle undesirable.

Eyes: Medium-sized, almond-shaped, never protruding. Dark brown preferred, lighter shade permissible, provided expression good and general harmony of head not destroyed. Expression lively, intelligent and self-assured.

Ears: Medium-sized, firm in texture, broad at base, set high, carried erect, almost parallel, never pulled inwards or tipped, tapering to a point, open at front. Never hanging. Folding back during movement permissible.

Mouth: Jaws strongly developed. With a perfect, regular and complete scissor bite, i.e. upper teeth closely overlapping lower teeth and set square to the jaw. Teeth healthy and strong. Full dentition desirable.

Neck: Fairly long, strong, with well developed muscles, free from throatiness. Carried at 45 degrees angle to horizontal, raised when excited, lowered at fast trot.

Forequarters: Shoulder blades long, set obliquely (45 degrees) laid flat to body. Upper arm strong, well muscled, joining shoulder blade at approximately 90 degrees. Forelegs straight from pasterns to elbows viewed from any angle, bone oval rather than round. Pasterns firm, supple and slightly angulated. Elbows neither tucked in nor turned out. Length of foreleg exceeding depth of chest.

Body: Length measured from point of breast bone to rear edge of pelvis, exceeding height at withers. Correct ratio 10 to 9 or 8 and a half. Undersized dogs, stunted growth, high-legged dogs, those too heavy or too light in build, overloaded fronts, too short overall appearance, any feature detracting from reach or endurance of gait, undesirable. Chest

An example of a typical German-bred dog.

27

deep (45-48 percent) of height at shoulder, not too broad, brisket long, well developed. Ribs well formed and long; neither barrel-shaped nor too flat; allowing free movement of elbows when gaiting. Relatively short loin. Belly firm, only slightly drawn up. Back between withers and croup, straight, strongly developed, not too long. Overall length achieved by correct angle of well laid shoulders, correct length of croup and hindquarters. Withers long, of good height and well defined, joining back in a smooth line without disrupting flowing topline, slightly sloping from front to back. Weak, soft and roach backs undesirable and should be rejected. Loin broad, strong, well muscled. Croup long, gently curving downwards to tail without disrupting flowing topline. Short, steep or flat croups undesirable.

Hindquarters: Overall strong, broad and well muscled, enabling effortless for-

All-black German Shepherd Dogs are acceptable according to the Kennel Club Standard, yet they cannot be shown on the Continent.

ward propulsion of whole body. Upper thighbone, viewed from side, sloping to slightly longer lower thighbone. Hind angulation sufficient if imaginary line dropped from point of buttocks cuts through lower thigh just in front of hock, continuing down slightly in front of hindfeet. Angulations corresponding approximately with front angulation, without over-angulation, hock strong. Any tendency towards over-angulation of hindquarters reduces firmness and endurance.

Feet: Rounded toes well closed and arched. Pads well cushioned and durable. Nails short, strong and dark in colour. Dewclaws removed from hindlegs.

Tail: Bushy-haired, reaches at least to hock—ideal length reaching to middle of metatarsus. At rest tail hangs in slight sabre-like curve; when moving raised and curve increased, ideally never above level of back. Short, rolled, curled, generally carried badly or stumpy from birth, undesirable.

Gait/Movement: Sequence of step follows diagonal pattern, moving foreleg and opposite hindleg forward simultaneously; hindfoot thrust forward to midpoint of body and having equally long reach with forefeet without any noticeable change in backline.

Coat: Outer coat consisting of straight, hard, close-lying hair as dense as possible; thick undercoat. Hair on head, ears, front of legs, paws and toes short; on back longer and thicker; in some males forming slight ruff. Hair longer on back of legs as far down as pasterns and stifles and forming fairly thick trousers on hindquarters. No hard and fast rule for length of hair; mole-type coats undesirable.

Colour: Black or black saddle with tan, or gold to light grey markings. All black, all grey, with lighter or brown markings referred to as Sables. Nose black. Light markings on chest or very pale colour on inside of legs permissible but undesirable, as are whitish nails, red-tipped tails or wishy-washy faded colours defined as lacking in pigmentation. Blues, livers, albinos, whites (i.e. almost pure white dogs with black noses) and near whites *highly undesirable.* Undercoat, except in all black dogs, usually grey or fawn.

Colour in itself is of secondary importance having no effect on character or fitness for work. Final colour of a young dog only ascertained when outer coat has developed.

Size: Ideal height (from withers and just touching elbows): dogs: 62.5 cms (25 ins); bitches: 57.5 cms (23 ins). 2.5 cms (1 in) either above or below ideal permissible.

Faults: Any departure from the foregoing points should be considered a fault and the seriousness with which the fault should be regarded should be in exact proportion to its degree. *Note:* Male animals should have two apparently normal testicles fully descended into the scrotum.

English Champion Mortoff Marcus represents the desirable breed type. This dog is the sire of the famous English Champion Norwulk Going for Gold of Slatehouse, owned by Gary Grey.

	CORRECT	**INCORRECT**

EARS

Should be held erect and parallel, not turned in.

BITE

Teeth should meet in a scissors bite, jaw should not be undershot.

FOREQUARTERS

Forelegs should be straight from pasterns to elbows when viewed from any angle.

CROUP

Should gently curve down to tail in a flowing line; should not be short, steep or flat.

HINDQUARTERS

Angulation in proportion to front angulation, with strong hock. Over-angulation reduces firmness and endurance.

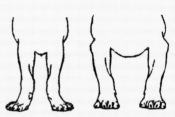

FEET

Should be rounded and arched, nails short and dark.

It's hard to determine a young pup's show potential. It's best to evaluate his conformation after he has gone through the awkward stages of growth.

A well-bred German Shepherd is a sight to behold. Look for a healthy, alert pup to grow into a faithful guardian and companion.

Your German Shepherd Puppy

OWNER CONSIDERATIONS

Although the reader of these pages is more likely interested in finding a companionable and family animal than a show champion, there remain many serious factors governing your choice. A primary consideration is time, not only the time of the animal's allotted life span, which is well over ten years, but also of the time required for the owner to exercise and care for the creature. If you are not committed to the welfare and whole existence of this energetic, purposeful animal; if, in the simplest, most basic example, you are not willing to walk your dog daily, despite the weather, do not choose a German Shepherd Dog as a companion.

Space is another important consideration. The German Shepherd Dog in early puppyhood may be well accommodated in a corner of your kitchen but after only six

All German Shepherd puppies are lovable dogs. Don't let your heart make the selection...use your head.

months when the dog is likely over 60 pounds, larger space certainly will be required. A garden with a fence is also a basic and reasonable expectation.

Along with these factors there are the usual problems associated with puppies of any breed like the damages likely to be sustained by your floors, furniture, flowers and, not least of all, to your freedom (of movement), as in holiday or weekend trips. This union is a serious affair and should be deeply considered but once decided, your choice of a German Shepherd

---

DID YOU KNOW?
Your puppy should have a well-fed appearance but not a distended abdomen, which may indicate worms or incorrect feeding, or both. The body should be firm, with a solid feel. The skin of the abdomen should be pale pink and clean, without signs of scratching or rash. Check the hind legs to make certain that dewclaws were removed, if any were present at birth.

Dog is, perhaps, the most rewarding of all breeds. A few suggestions will help in the purchase of your dog.

Selecting the German Shepherd puppy is NOT an easy task. The physical characteristics are easy to evaluate, it is matching your temperament with that of the dog that is difficult.

ACQUIRING A PUPPY

The safest method of obtaining your puppy is to seek out a local reputable breeder. This is suggested even if you are not looking for a show specimen. The novice breeders and pet owners who advertise at attractive prices in the local newspapers are probably kind enough towards their dogs, but perhaps do not have the expertise or facilities required to successfully raise these animals. These pet puppies are frequently badly weaned and left with the mother too long without the supplemental feeding required by this fast growing breed. This lack of proper feeding can cause indigestion, rickets, weak bones, poor teeth and other problems. Veterinary bills may soon distort initial savings into financial, or worse, emotional loss.

Inquire about inoculations and when the puppy was last dosed for worms. Check the ears. Although many puppies do not have erect ears until five or six months, some move-

ment forward and signs of lifting when the puppy is alerted are good predictors of normal development.

Colour is a matter of personal choice, but whatever colour you prefer, your puppy should have a dark nose and, preferably, dark toenails. This is a consideration of pigmentation, which should not be confused with colour. Colour in German Shepherd Dogs generally becomes lighter, so it is wise to choose a puppy with

DID YOU KNOW?

Two important documents you will get from the breeder are the pup's pedigree and registration papers. The breeder should register the litter and each pup with The Kennel Club, and it is necessary for you to have the paperwork if you plan on showing or breeding in the future.

Make sure you know the breeder's intentions on which type of registration he will obtain for the pup. There are limited registrations which may prohibit the dog from being shown or from competing in non-conformation trials such as Working or Agility if the breeder feels that the pup is not of sufficient quality to do so. There is also a type of registration that will permit the dog in non-conformation competition only.

If your dog is registered with a Kennel-Club-recognised breed club, then you can register the pup with The Kennel Club yourself. Your breeder can assist you with the specifics of the registration process.

deep rich pigmentation and as much black as possible. Dark eyes are best in any colour. Look for expression in your puppy's eyes, as this is a good sign of intelligence.

Note the way your choice moves. The German Shepherd Dog, even in puppyhood, should show light and swift movement with no tendency to stumble or drag the hind feet. Look at the mouth to make sure that the bite is fairly even, although maturity can often correct errors present at puppyhood. If you have any doubts, ask to see the parents' mouths. This brings up an important point—do not

---

DID YOU KNOW?

Another important consideration remains to be discussed and that is the sex of your puppy. For a family companion, a German Shepherd Dog bitch is the best choice, considering the female's inbred concern for all young creatures and her accompanying tolerance and patience. If you do not intend to spay your pet when she has matured or is well over her growing period, then extra care is required during the biannual periods of heat.

---

purchase a puppy without first seeing at least one of the parents.

Male dogs of this breed are equally devoted and loyal but have the drawback of being in season all year and, therefore, prone to possible wandering. This is the central reason why females are always chosen as guide dogs for the blind.

COMMITMENT OF OWNERSHIP
After considering all of these factors, you have most likely already made some very important decisions about

selecting your puppy. You have chosen a German Shepherd, which means that you have decided which characteristics you want in a dog and what type of dog will best fit into your family and lifestyle. If you have selected a breeder, you have gone a step further—you have done your research and found a responsible, conscientious person who breeds quality German Shepherds and who should be a reliable source of help as you and your puppy adjust to life together. If you have observed a litter in action, you have gotten a firsthand look at the

The best place to start looking for a German Shepherd puppy is at the kennel of a reputable local breeder.

Winning Police Dog Action for 1999 is Overhills Foggarty, with WPC Leigh White, and Police National Champion 1999, Overhills Pettifoger with PC Andy Lloyd. Both of these winners bred by Meg Purnell-Carpenter.

35

dynamics of a puppy 'pack' and, thus, you have gotten to learn about each pup's individual personality—perhaps you have even found one that particularly appeals to you.

Are you prepared for the new puppy?

However, even if you have not yet found the German Shepherd puppy of your dreams, observing pups will help you learn to recognise certain behaviour and to determine what a pup's behaviour indicates about his temperament. You will be able to pick out which pups are the leaders, which ones are less outgoing, which ones are confident, which ones are shy, playful, friendly, aggressive, etc. Equally as important, you will learn to recognise what a healthy pup should look and act like. All of these things will help you in your search, and when you find the German Shepherd that was meant for you, you will know it!

Researching your breed, selecting a responsible breeder and observing as many pups as possible are all important steps on the way to dog ownership. It may seem like a lot of effort...and you have not even brought the pup home yet! Remember, though, you cannot be too careful when it comes to deciding on the type of dog you want and finding out about your prospective pup's background. Buying a puppy is not—or should not be—just another whimsical purchase. In fact, this is one instance in which you actually *do* get to choose your own family! But, you may be thinking, buying a puppy should be fun—it should not be so serious and so much work. If you keep in mind the thought that your puppy is not a cuddly stuffed toy or decorative lawn ornament, but instead will become a real member of your family, you will realise that while buying a puppy is a pleasurable and exciting endeavour, it is not something to be taken lightly. Relax...the fun will start when the pup comes home!

Always keep in mind that a puppy is nothing more than a baby in a furry disguise...a baby who is virtually helpless in a human world and who trusts his owner for fulfillment of his basic needs for survival. That goes beyond food, water and shelter; your pup needs care, protection, guidance and love. If you are not prepared to commit to this, then you are not prepared to own a dog.

> **DID YOU KNOW?**
> The cost of food must also be mentioned. This is not a breed that can be maintained on table scraps and light supplement. German Shepherd Dogs need a good supply of protein to develop the bone and muscle required in a working animal. German Shepherd Dogs are not picky eaters but unless fed properly they can quickly succumb to skin problems.

Wait a minute, you say. How hard could this be? All of my neighbours own dogs and they seem to be doing just fine. Why should I have to worry about all of this? Well, you *should not* worry about it; in fact, you will probably find that once your German Shepherd pup gets used to his new home, he will fall into his place in the family quite naturally. But it never hurts to emphasise the commitment of dog ownership. With some time and patience, it is really not too difficult to raise a curious and exuberant German Shepherd pup to be a well-adjusted and well-mannered adult dog—a dog that could be your most loyal friend.

PREPARING PUPPY'S PLACE IN YOUR HOME

Researching your breed and finding a breeder are only two aspects of the 'homework' you will have to do before bringing your German Shepherd puppy home. You will also have to prepare your home and family for the new addition. Much like you would prepare a nursery for a newborn baby, you will need to designate a place in your home that will be the

puppy's own. How you prepare your home will depend on how much freedom the dog will be allowed: will he be confined to one room or a specific area in the house, or will he be allowed to roam as he pleases? Will he spend most of his time in the house or will he be primarily an outdoor dog? Whatever you decide, you must ensure that he has a place that he can 'call his own.'

When you bring your new puppy into your home, you are bringing him into what will become his home as well. Obviously, you did not buy a puppy so that he could take over your house, but in order for a puppy to grow into a stable, well-adjusted dog, he has to feel comfortable in his sur-

Pet shops offer a wide range of styles and sizes of crates. Use them in training and for your dog's safety—they are NOT cruel.

Your dog should be able to stand comfortably in his crate. This crate is not high enough especially since this young German Shepherd still has growing to do.

37

cruel—crates have many humane and highly effective uses in dog care and training. For example, crate training is a very popular and very successful housebreaking method; a crate can keep your dog safe during travel; and, perhaps most importantly, a crate provides your dog with a place of his own in your home. It serves as a 'doggie bedroom' of sorts—your German Shepherd can curl up in his crate when he wants to sleep or when he just needs a break. Many dogs sleep in their crates overnight. When lined with soft blankets and with a favourite toy placed inside, a crate becomes a cosy pseudo-den for your dog. Like his ancestors, he too will seek out the comfort and retreat of a den—you just happen to be providing him with something a little more luxurious than leaves and twigs lining a dirty ditch.

By studying the litter in action you should be able to pick out the pup that best suits your personality.

roundings. Remember, he is leaving the warmth and security of his mother and littermates, plus the familiarity of the only place he has ever known, so it is important to make his transition as easy as possible. By preparing a place in your home for the puppy, you are making him feel as welcome as possible in a strange new place. It should not take him long to get used to it, but the sudden shock of being transplanted is somewhat traumatic for a young pup. Imagine how a small child would feel in the same situation—that is how your puppy must be feeling. It is up to you to reassure him and to let him know, 'Little fellow, you are going to like it here!'

As far as purchasing a crate, the type that you buy is up to you. It will most likely be one of the two most popular types: wire or fibreglass.

Crate training a Shepherd puppy can be fun for the pup and the owner. This pup seems to be having a grand time making himself comfortable.

WHAT YOU SHOULD BUY
CRATE
To someone unfamiliar with the use of crates in dog training, it may seem like punishment to shut a dog in a crate; this is not the case at all. Crates *are not*

DID YOU KNOW?

Unfortunately, when a puppy is purchased by someone who does not take into consideration the time and attention that dog ownership requires, it is the puppy who suffers when he is either abandoned or placed in a shelter by a frustrated owner. So all of the 'homework' you do in preparation for your pup's arrival will benefit you both. The more informed you are, the more you will know what to expect and the better equipped you will be to handle the ups and downs of raising a puppy. Hopefully, everyone in the household is willing to do his part in raising and caring for the pup. The anticipation of owning a dog often brings a lot of promises from excited family members: 'I will walk him every day,' 'I will feed him,' 'I will housebreak him,' etc., but these things take time and effort, and promises can easily be forgotten once the novelty of the new pet has worn off.

There are advantages and disadvantages to each type. For example, a wire crate is more open, allowing the air to flow through and affording the dog a view of what is going on around him. A fibreglass crate, however, is sturdier and can double as a travel crate since it provides more protection for the dog. The size of the crate is another thing to consider. Puppies do not stay puppies forever—in fact, sometimes it seems as if they grow right before your eyes. A Yorkie-sized crate may be fine for a very young German Shepherd pup, but it will not do him much good for long! Unless you have the money and the inclination to buy a new crate every time your pup has a growth spurt, it is better to get one that will accommodate your dog both as a pup and at full size. A large crate will be necessary for a full-grown German Shepherd, as their approximate weight range is between 65 and 95 pounds.

BEDDING

Veterinary bedding in the dog's crate will help the dog feel more at home. First, the bedding will take the place of the leaves, twigs, etc., that the pup would use in the wild to make a den; the pup can make his own 'burrow' in the crate. Although your pup is far removed from his den-making ancestors, the denning instinct is still a part of his genetic makeup. Second, until you bring your pup home, he has been sleeping amidst the warmth of his mother and littermates, and while a blanket is not the same as a warm,

Your pet shop should have all the supplies you will require for your new German Shepherd puppy. Buy these supplies BEFORE THE PUPPY ARRIVES.

breathing body, it still provides heat and something with which to snuggle. You will want to wash your pup's blankets frequently in case he has an

Get a crate large enough for your growing dog.

accident in his crate, and replace or remove any blanket that becomes ragged and starts to fall apart.

TOYS

Toys are a must for dogs of all ages, especially for curious playful pups. Puppies are the 'children' of the dog world, and what child does not love toys? Chew toys provide enjoyment to

Pet shops offer all kinds of toys. German Shepherd puppies have strong jaws, so make sure that the toys you purchase will withstand heavy chewing.

both dog and owner—your dog will enjoy playing with his favourite toys, while you will enjoy the fact that they distract him from your expensive shoes and leather sofa. Puppies love to chew; in fact, chewing is a physical

need for pups as they are teething, and everything looks appetising! The full range of your possessions—from old dishrag to Oriental rug—are fair game in the eyes of a teething pup. Puppies are not all that discerning when it comes to finding something to literally 'sink their teeth into'—everything tastes great!

Stuffed toys are another option; these are good to put in the dog's crate to give him some company. Be careful of these, as a pup can de-stuff one pretty quickly, and stay away from stuffed toys with small plastic eyes or parts that a pup could choke on. Similarly, squeaky

---

DID YOU KNOW?

During crate training, you should partition off the section of the crate in which the pup stays. If he is given too big of an area, this will hinder your training efforts. Crate training is based on the fact that a dog does not like to soil his sleeping quarters, so it is ineffective to keep a pup in a crate that is so big that he can eliminate in one end and get far enough away from it to sleep. Also, you want to make the crate den-like for the pup. Blankets and toys will make the crate cosy for the small German Shepherd; as he grows, you may want to evict some of his 'roommates' to make more room.

It will take some coaxing at first, but be patient. Given some time to get used to it, your pup will adapt to his new home-within-a-home quite nicely.

---

toys are quite popular. There are dogs that will come running from anywhere in the house at the first sound from their favourite squeaky friend. Again, if a pup de-stuffs one of these, the small plastic squeaker inside can be dangerous if swallowed. Monitor the condition of your pup's toys carefully and get rid of any that have been chewed to the point of becoming potentially dangerous.

Be careful of natural bones, which have a tendency to splinter into sharp, dangerous pieces. Also be careful of rawhide, which after enough chewing can turn into pieces

DID YOU KNOW?

With a big variety of dog toys available, and so many that look like they would be a lot of fun for a dog, be careful in your selection. It is amazing what a set of puppy teeth can do to an innocent-looking toy, so, obviously, safety is a major consideration. Be sure to choose the most durable products that you can find. This is an especially important consideration with a breed like the German Shepherd who has naturally strong teeth and jaws. Hard nylon bones and toys are a safe bet, and many of them are offered in different scents and flavours that will be sure to capture your German Shepherd's attention. It is always fun to play a game of catch with your dog, and there are balls and flying discs that are specially made to withstand dog teeth.

that are easy to swallow, and also watch out for the mushy mess it can turn into on your carpet.

Your dog should seek refuge in his crate. It should not be used for punishment.

LEAD

A nylon lead is probably the best option as it is the most resistant to puppy teeth should your pup take a liking to chewing on his lead. Of course, this is a habit that should be nipped in the bud, but if your pup likes to chew on his lead he has a very slim chance of being able to chew through the strong nylon. Nylon leads are also lightweight, which is good for a young German Shepherd who is just getting used to the idea of walking on a lead. For everyday walking and safety purposes, the nylon lead is a good choice. As your pup grows up and gets used to walking on the lead, and can do it politely, you may want to purchase a flexible lead, which allows you either to extend the length to give the dog a broader area to explore or to pull in the lead when you want to keep him close. Of course there are special leads for training purposes, and specially made leather harnesses for the working German Shepherd, but these are not necessary for routine walks. If your German

Shepherd is especially strong or tends to pull on the lead, you may want to purchase something stronger, like a thicker leather lead.

COLLAR

Your pup should get used to wearing a collar all the time since you will want to attach his ID tags to his collar. Also, the lead and collar go hand in hand— you have to attach the lead to something! A lightweight nylon collar will be a good choice; make sure that it fits snugly enough so that the pup cannot wriggle out of it, but loose enough so that it will not be uncomfortably tight around the pup's neck. You should be able to fit a finger in between the pup and the collar. It may take some time for your pup to get used to wearing the collar, but soon he will not even notice that it is there. Choke collars are made for training, but should only be used by an owner who knows exactly how to use it. If you use a stronger leather lead or a chain lead to walk your German Shepherd, you will need a stronger collar as well.

FOOD AND WATER BOWLS

Your pup will need two bowls, one for food and one for water. You may want two sets of bowls, one for inside and one for outside, depending on where the dog will be fed and where he will be spending most of his time. Stainless steel or sturdy plastic bowls are popular choices. Although plastic bowls are more chewable, dogs tend not to chew on the steel variety, which can also be sanitised. Some dog owners like to put their dogs' food and water bowls on a specially made elevated stand; this brings the food closer to the dog's level so he does not have to bend down as far, thus aiding his digestion and helping to guard against bloat or gastric torsion in deep-chested dogs. The most important thing is to buy sturdy bowls since, again, anything is in danger of being chewed by puppy teeth and you do not want your dog to be constantly chewing apart his bowl (for his safety and for your wallet!).

CLEANING SUPPLIES

A pup that is not housetrained means you will be doing a lot of cleaning until he is. Accidents will occur, which is okay for now because he does not know any better. All you can do is clean up any 'accidents'—old rags, towels, newspapers and a safe disinfectant are good to have on hand.

Pet shops offer many types of dog tags. Have one engraved with all of the necessary information and attach it securely to your German Shepherd's collar.

BEYOND THE BASICS

The items previously discussed are the bare necessities. You will find out what else you need as you go along—grooming supplies, flea/tick protection, baby gates to partition a room, etc.—these things will vary depending on your situation. It is just important that right away you have everything you need to feed and make your German Shepherd comfortable in his first few days at home.

PUPPY-PROOFING YOUR HOME

Aside from making sure that your German Shepherd will be comfortable in your home, you also have to make sure that your home is safe for your German Shepherd. This means taking precautions to make sure that your pup will not get into anything he should not get into and that there is nothing within his reach that may harm him should he

> **DID YOU KNOW?**
> You will probably start feeding your German Shepherd pup the same food that he has been getting from the breeder; the breeder should give you a few days' supply to start you off. Although you should not give your pup too many treats, you will want to have puppy treats on hand for coaxing, training, rewards, etc. Be careful, though, as a small pup's calorie requirements are relatively low and a few treats can add up to almost a full day's worth of calories without the required nutrition.

sniff it, chew it, inspect it, etc. This probably seems obvious since, while you are primarily concerned with your pup's safety, at the same time you do not want your belongings to be ruined. Breakables should be placed out of reach if your dog is to have full run of the house. If he is to be limited to certain places within the house, keep any potentially dangerous items in the 'off-limits' areas. An electrical cord can pose a danger should the puppy decide to taste it—and who is going to convince a pup that it would not make a great chew toy? Cords should be routed under the carpeting or fastened tightly against the wall. If your dog is going to spend time in a crate, make sure that there is nothing near his crate that he can reach if he sticks his curious little nose or paws through the openings. And just as you would with a child, keep all household cleaners and chemicals where the pup cannot get to them.

German Shepherd Dogs must ALWAYS have water available. Obtain a water bowl and keep it clean and full of fresh water.

Before you bring your German Shepherd puppy home, you should purchase all of the necessary paraphernalia. Anticipate the needs of a growing dog and be prepared!

43

Properly supervise your pup when he is out exploring the garden. Many plants and bushes can be dangerous to a young pup.

It is just as important to make sure that the outside of your home is safe. Of course your puppy should never be unsupervised, but a pup let loose in the garden will want to run and explore, and he should be granted that freedom. Do not let a fence give you a false sense of security; you would be surprised how crafty (and persistent) a dog can be in figuring out how to dig under and squeeze his way through small holes, or to jump or climb over a fence. The remedy is to make the fence high enough so that it really is impossible for your dog

Puppy-proof your house *before* the puppy comes home.

Be sure that you have removed all potentially poisonous vegetation from your garden. Nothing will deter your curious pup from sampling and playing in everything he can find.

to get over it (about 3 metres should suffice), and well embedded into the ground. Be sure to repair or secure any gaps in the fence. Check the fence periodically to ensure that it is in good shape and make repairs as needed; a very determined pup may return to the same spot to 'work on it' until he is able to get through.

FIRST TRIP TO THE VET
Okay, you have picked out your puppy, your home and family are ready, now all you have to do is pick your German Shepherd up from the breeder and the fun begins, right? Well…not so fast. Something else you need to prepare for is your pup's first trip to the veterinary

surgeon. Perhaps the breeder can recommend someone in the area that specialises in German Shepherds, or maybe you know some other German Shepherd owners who can suggest a good vet. Either way, you should have an appointment arranged for your pup before you pick him up; plan on taking him for a checkup within the first few days of bringing him home.

The pup's first visit will consist of an overall examination to make sure that the pup does not have any problems that are not apparent to the eye. The veterinary surgeon will also set up a schedule for the pup's vaccinations; the

POISONOUS PLANTS

Below is a partial list of plants that are considered poisonous. These plants can cause skin irritation, illness, and even death. You should be aware of the types of plants that grow in your garden and that you keep in your home. Special care should be taken to rid your garden of dangerous plants and to keep all plants in the household out of your German Shepherd's reach.

American Blue Flag
Bachelor's Button
Barberry
Bog Iris
Boxwood
Buttercup
Cherry Pits
Chinese Arbor
Chokecherry
Christmas Rose
Climbing Lily
Crown of Thorns
Elderberry (berries)
Elephant Ear
English Ivy
False Acacia
Fern
Foxglove
Hellebore
Herb of Grace
Holly
Horse Chestnut
Iris (bulb)

Japanese Yew
Jerusalem Cherry
Jimson Weed
Lenten Rose
Lily of the Valley
Marigold
Milkwort
Mistletoe (berries)
Monkshood
Mullein
Narcissus
Peony
Persian Ivy
Rhododendron
Rhubarb
Shallon
Siberian Iris
Solomon's Seal
Star of Bethlehem
Water Lily
Wood Spurge
Wisteria
Yew

This young Shepherd gets on well with the family's two Tibetan Spaniels. If properly introduced, your Shepherd can be quite gregarious with all members of the household.

breeder will inform you of which ones the pup has already received and the vet can continue from there.

INTRODUCTION TO THE FAMILY

Everyone in the house will be excited about the puppy coming home and will want to pet him and play with him, but it is best to make the introduction low-key so as not to overwhelm the puppy. He is apprehensive already; it is the first time he has been separated from his mother and the breeder, and the ride to your home is likely the first time he has been in an auto. The last thing you want to do is smother him, as this will only

Take your dog to the vet as soon as possible. Especially check for worms that are transmissible to humans.

frighten him further. This is not to say that human contact is not extremely necessary at this stage, because this is the time when an instant connection between the pup and his human family are formed. Gentle petting and soothing words should help console him, as well as just putting him down and letting him explore on his own (under your watchful eye, of course).

The pup may approach the family members or may busy himself with exploring for awhile. Gradually, each person should spend some time with the pup, one at a time, crouching down to get as close to the pup's

DID YOU KNOW?
Many good breeders will offer you insurance with your new puppy, which is an excellent idea. The first few weeks of insurance will probably be covered free of charge or with only minimal cost, allowing you to take up the policy when this expires. If you own a pet dog, it is sensible to take out such a policy as veterinary fees can be high, although routine vaccinations and boosters are not covered. Look carefully at the many options open to you before deciding which suits best. Your breeder or other dog owners may be able to give you advice.

level as possible and letting him sniff their hands and petting him gently. He definitely needs human attention and he needs to be touched—this is how to form an immediate bond. Just remember that the pup is experiencing a lot of things for the first time, all at the same time. There are new people, new noises, new smells, and new things to investigate; so be gentle, be affectionate and be as comforting as you can be.

YOUR PUP'S FIRST NIGHT HOME

You have travelled home with your new charge safely in his basket or crate. He's been to the vet for a thorough check-over; he's been weighed, his papers examined; perhaps he's even been vaccinated and wormed as well. He's met the family, licked the whole family, including the excited children and the less-than-happy cat. He's explored his area, his new bed, the garden and anywhere else he's been permitted. He's eaten his first meal at home and relieved himself in the proper place. He's heard lots of new sounds, smelled new friends and seen more of the outside world than ever before.

That was the just the first day! He's tuckered out and is ready for bed…or so you think!

It's puppy's first night and you are ready to say 'Good night'—keep in mind that this is puppy's first night ever to be sleeping alone. His dam and littermates are no longer at paw's length away and he's a bit scared, cold and lonely. Be reassuring to your new family member. This is not the time to spoil him and give in to his inevitable whining.

Puppies whine. They whine to let the others know where they are and hopefully to get company out of it.

Place your pup in his new bed or crate in his room and close the door. Mercifully, he will fall asleep without a peep. If the inevitable occurs, ignore the whining; he is fine. Be strong and keep his interest in mind. Do not allow your heart to become guilty and visit the pup. He will fall asleep.

Curiosity is a way of life for all puppies. This pup seems anxious to meet new friends and see the world.

Many breeders recommend placing a piece of bedding from his former homestead in his new bed so that he recognises the scent of his littermates. Others still advise placing a hot water bottle in his bed for warmth. This latter may be a good idea provided the pup doesn't attempt to suckle—he'll get good and wet and may not fall asleep so fast.

Puppy's first night can be somewhat stressful for the pup and his new family. Remember that you are setting the tone of nighttime at your house. Unless you want to play with

47

Have your German Shepherd puppy meet and socialise with his new family, especially the children. The children must be instructed in the proper care and handling of the puppy.

your pup every evening at 10 p.m., midnight and 2 a.m., don't initiate the habit. Surely your family will thank you, and so will your pup!

PREVENTING PUPPY PROBLEMS

Socialisation

Now that you have done all of the preparatory work and have helped your pup get accustomed to his new home and family, it is about time for you to have some fun! Socialising your German Shepherd pup gives you the opportunity to show off your new friend, and your pup gets to reap the benefits of being an adorable furry creature that people will coo over, want to pet and, in general, think is absolutely precious!

Besides getting to know his new family, your puppy should be exposed to other people, animals and situations. This will help him become well adjusted as he grows up and less prone to being timid or fearful of the new things he will encounter. Your pup's socialisation began at the breeder's, now it is your responsibility to continue. The socialisation he receives up until the age of 12 weeks is the most critical, as this is the time when he forms his impressions of the outside world. Lack of socialisation can manifest itself in fear and aggression as the dog grows up. He needs lots of human interaction, affection, handling and exposure to other animals. Be careful during the eight-to-ten-week period, also known as the fear period. The interaction he receives during this time should be gentle and reassuring.

Once your pup has received his necessary vaccinations, feel free to take him out and about (on his lead, of course). Take him around the neighbourhood, take him on your daily errands, let people pet him, let him meet other dogs and pets, etc. Puppies do not have to try to make friends; there will be no shortage of people who will want to introduce themselves. Just make sure that you carefully supervise each interaction. If the neighbourhood children want to say hello, for example, that is great—children and pups most often make great companions. But sometimes an excited child can unintentionally handle a pup too roughly, or an overzealous pup can playfully nip a little too hard. You want to make socialisation experiences positive ones; what a pup learns during this very formative stage will impact his attitude toward future encounters. A pup that has a bad experience with a child may grow up to be a dog that is shy around or aggressive toward children, and you want your dog to be comfortable around everyone.

Play can be defined as supervised mischief! This playful pup may have a promising future in gardening.

CONSISTENCY IN TRAINING

Dogs, being pack animals, naturally need a leader, or else they try to establish dominance in their packs. When you bring a dog into your family, who becomes the leader and who becomes the 'pack' are entirely up to you! Your pup's intuitive quest for dominance, coupled with the fact that it is nearly impossible to look at

---

DID YOU KNOW?

Thorough socialisation includes not only meeting new people but also being introduced to new experiences such as riding in the auto, having his coat brushed, hearing the television, walking in a crowd—the list is endless. The more your pup experiences, and the more positive the experiences are, the less of a shock and the less scary it will be for your pup to encounter new things.

---

an adorable German Shepherd pup, with his 'puppy-dog' eyes and his too-big-for his-head-still-floppy ears, and not cave in, give the pup almost an unfair advantage in getting the upper hand! And a pup will definitely test the waters to see what he can and cannot get away with. Do not give in to those pleading eyes—stand your ground when it comes to disciplining the pup and make sure that all family members do the same. It will only confuse the pup when Mother tells him to get off the couch when he is used to sitting up there with Father to watch the nightly news. Avoid discrepancies by having all members of the household decide on the rules before the pup even comes home...and *be consistent* in enforcing them! Early training shapes the dog's personality, so you cannot be unclear in what you expect.

COMMON PUPPY PROBLEMS

The best way to prevent problems is to be proactive in stopping an undesirable behaviour as soon as it starts. The old saying 'You can't teach an old dog new tricks' does not necessarily hold true, but it is true that it is much easier to discourage bad behaviour in a young developing pup than to wait until the pup's bad behaviour becomes the adult dog's bad habit. There are some problems that are especially prevalent in puppies as they develop.

Bad behaviour can be cured more easily in puppies than adult dogs.

NIPPING

As puppies start to teethe, they feel the need to sink their teeth into anything...unfortunately that includes your fingers, arms, hair, toes...whatever happens to be available. You may find this behaviour cute for about the first five seconds...until you feel just how sharp those puppy teeth are. This is something you want to discourage immediately and consistently with a firm 'No!' (or whatever number of firm 'No's' it takes for him to understand that you mean business) and replace your finger with an appropriate chew toy. While this behaviour is merely annoying when the dog is still young, it can become

Do not allow your pup to chew on your shoes or trouser leg. This will lead to problems later in life.

dangerous as your German Shepherd's adult teeth grow in and his jaws develop, if he thinks that it is okay to gnaw on human appendages. You do not want to take a chance with a German Shepherd, this is a breed whose jaws become naturally very strong. He does not mean any harm with a

DID YOU KNOW?

Chewing goes hand in hand with nipping in the sense that a teething puppy is always looking for a way to soothe his aching gums. In this case, instead of chewing on you, he may have taken a liking to your favourite shoe or something else which he should not be chewing. Again, realise that this is a normal canine behaviour that does not need to be discouraged, only redirected. Your pup just needs to be taught what is acceptable to chew on and what is off limits. Consistently tell him NO when you catch him chewing on something forbidden and give him a chew toy. Conversely, praise him when you catch him chewing on something appropriate. In this way you are discouraging the inappropriate behaviour and reinforcing the desired behaviour. The puppy chewing should stop after his adult teeth have come in, but most adult dogs continue to chew for various reasons—perhaps because he is bored, perhaps to relieve tension, or perhaps he just likes to chew. That is why it is important to redirect his chewing when he is still young.

friendly nip, but he also does not know his own strength.

CRYING/WHINING

Your pup will often cry, whine, whimper, howl or make some type of commotion when he is left alone. This is basically his way of calling out for attention, of calling out to make sure that you know he is there and that you have not forgotten about him. He feels insecure when he is left alone, for example, when you are out of the house and he is in his crate or when you are in another part of the house and he cannot see you. The noise he is making is an expression of the anxiety he feels at being alone, so he needs to be taught that being alone is okay. You are not actually training the dog to stop making noise, you are training him to feel comfortable when he is alone and thus removing the need for him to make the noise. This is where the crate filled with cosy blankets and toys comes in

Your German Shepherd Dog will certainly make a splash in your family!

handy. You want to know that he is safe when you are not there to supervise, and you know that he will be safe in his crate rather than roaming freely about the house. In order for the pup to stay in his crate without making a fuss, he needs to be comfortable in his crate. On that note, it is *extremely* important that the crate is *never* used as a form of punishment, or the pup will have a negative association with the crate.

Accustom the pup to the crate in short, gradually increasing time intervals in which you put him in the crate, maybe with a treat, and stay in the room with him. If he cries or makes a fuss, do not go to him, but stay in his sight. Gradually he will realise that staying in his crate is all right without your help, and it will not be so traumatic for him when you are not around. You may want to leave the radio on softly when you leave the house; the sound of human voices may be comforting to him.

DID YOU KNOW?

The majority of problems that are commonly seen in young pups will disappear as your German Shepherd gets older. However, how you deal with problems when he is young will determine how he reacts to discipline as an adult dog. It is important to establish who is boss (hopefully it will be you!) right away when you are first bonding with your German Shepherd. This bond will set the tone for the rest of your life together.

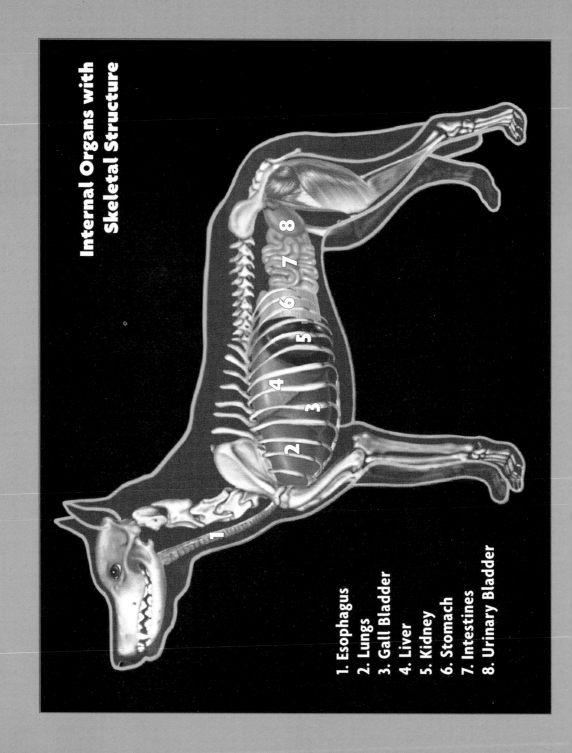

Internal Organs with Skeletal Structure

1. Esophagus
2. Lungs
3. Gall Bladder
4. Liver
5. Kidney
6. Stomach
7. Intestines
8. Urinary Bladder

Everyday Care of Your German Shepherd Dog

DIETARY AND FEEDING CONSIDERATIONS

You have probably heard it a thousand times, you are what you eat. Believe it or not, it's very true. For dogs, they are what you feed them because they have little choice in the matter. Even those people who truly want to feed their dogs the best often cannot do so because they do not know which foods are best for their dog.

Dog foods are produced in three basic types: dry, semi-moist and canned or tinned. Dry foods are for the cost conscious because they are much less expensive than semi-moist and canned. Dry foods contain the least fat and the most preservatives. Most tinned foods are 60-70-percent water, while semi-moist foods are so full of sugar that they are the least preferred by owners, though dogs welcome them (as does a child candy).

Three stages of development must be considered when selecting a diet

By the time German Shepherd puppies are eight weeks old they should be fed a puppy-formula dry food.

for your dog: the puppy stage, the mid-age or adult stage and the senior age or geriatric stage.

PUPPY STAGE

Puppies have a natural instinct to suck milk from their mother's breasts. They should exhibit this behaviour the first day of their lives. If they

Puppy foods are specially formulated to give puppies the nutrition they need during the crucial growth period.

don't suckle within a few hours you should attempt to put them onto their mother's nipple. Their failure to feed means you have to feed them yourself under the advice and guidance of a veterinary surgeon. This will involve a baby bottle and a special formula. Their mother's milk is much better than any formula because it contains colostrum, a sort of antibiotic milk which protects the puppy during the first eight to ten weeks of their lives.

Puppies should be allowed to nurse for six weeks and they should be slowly weaned away from their mother by introducing small portions of tinned meat after they are about one month old.

By the time they are eight weeks old, they should be completely weaned and fed solely a puppy dry food. During this weaning period, their diet is most important as the

The benefits of good nutrition will be evident in your German Shepherd Dog's shiny coat, alert demeanor and overall healthy appearance.

puppy grows fastest during its first year of life. Growth foods can be recommended by your veterinary surgeon and the puppy should be kept on this diet for up to 18 months.

Puppy diets should be balanced for your dog's needs and supplements of vitamins, minerals and protein should not be necessary.

ADULT DIETS

A dog is considered an adult when it has stopped growing. The growth is in height and/or length. Do not consider the dog's weight when the decision is made to switch from a puppy diet to a maintenance diet. Again you should rely upon your veterinary surgeon to recommend an acceptable maintenance diet. Major dog food manufacturers specialise in this type of food

and it is just necessary for you to select the one best suited to your dog's needs. Active dogs may have different requirements than sedate dogs.

A German Shepherd Dog reaches adulthood at about two years of age, though some dogs fully mature at 16 months, while others may take up to three years.

DIETS FOR SENIOR DOGS

As dogs get older, their metabolism changes. The older dog usually exercises less, moves more slowly and sleeps more. This change in lifestyle and physiological performance requires a change in diet. Since these changes take place slowly, they might not be recognizable. What is easily recognizable is weight gain. By continually feeding your dog an adult maintenance diet when it is slowing down metabolically, your dog will gain weight. Obesity in an older dog compounds the health problems that already accompany old age.

As your dog gets older, few of their organs function up to par. The kidneys slow down and the intestines become less efficient. These age-related factors are best handled with a change in diet and a change in feeding schedule to give smaller portions that are more easily digested.

There is no single best diet for every older dog. While many dogs do well on light or senior diets, other dogs do better on puppy diets or other special premium diets such as lamb and rice.

Be sensitive to your senior German

Water should be available to your German Shepherd at all times. Offering water in a bowl stand is an excellent way of guarding from bloat.

Shepherd Dog's diet and this will help control other problems that may arise with your old friend.

WATER

Just as your dog needs proper nutrition from his food, water is an essential 'nutrient' as well. Water keeps the dog's body properly hydrated and promotes normal function of the

> **DID YOU KNOW?**
>
> Many adult diets are based on grain. There is nothing wrong with this as long as it does not contain soy meal. Diets based on soy often cause flatulence (passing gas).
>
> Grain-based diets are almost always the least expensive and a good grain diet is just as good as the most expensive diet containing animal protein.
>
> There are many cases, however, when your dog might require a special diet. These special requirements should only be recommended by your veterinary surgeon.

What are you feeding your dog?

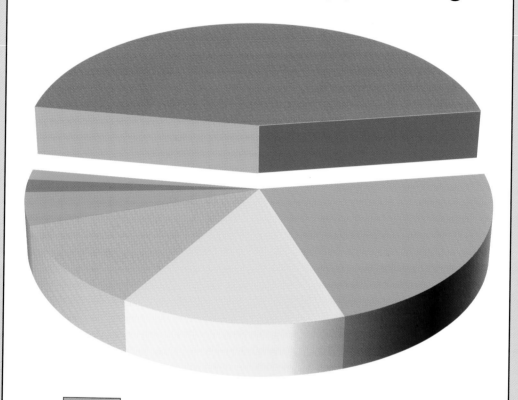

1.3% Calcium

1.6% Fatty Acids

4.6% Crude Fibre

11% Moisture

14% Crude Fat

22% Crude Protein

45.5% ? ? ?

Read the label on your dog food. Many dog foods only advise what 50—55% of the contents are, leaving the other 45% to doubt.

body's systems. During housebreaking it is necessary to keep an eye on how much water your German Shepherd is drinking, but once he is reliably trained he should have access to clean fresh water at all times. Make sure that the dog's water bowl is clean, and change the water often.

EXERCISE

All dogs require some form of exercise, regardless of breed. A sedentary lifestyle is as harmful to a dog as it is to a person. The German Shepherd happens to be an active breed that requires more exercise than, say, an English Bulldog, but you don't have to be a weightlifter or marathon runner to provide your dog with the exercise he needs. Regular walks, play sessions in the garden, or letting the dog run free in the garden under your supervision are all sufficient forms of exercise for the German Shepherd. For those who are more ambitious,

you will find that your German Shepherd will be able to keep up with you on extra long walks or the morning run. Not only is exercise essential to keep the dog's body fit, it is essential to his mental well-being. A bored dog will find something to do, which often manifests itself in some type of destructive behaviour. In this sense, it is essential for the owner's mental well-being as well!

GROOMING
BRUSHING

A natural bristle brush or a slicker brush can be used for regular routine brushing. Daily brushing is effective for removing dead hair and stimulating the dog's natural oils to add shine and a healthy look to the coat. Your German Shepherd is not a breed that needs excessive grooming, but his heavy coat needs to be brushed daily as part of routine maintenance. Daily brushing will

This German Shepherd pup knows how to cool off!

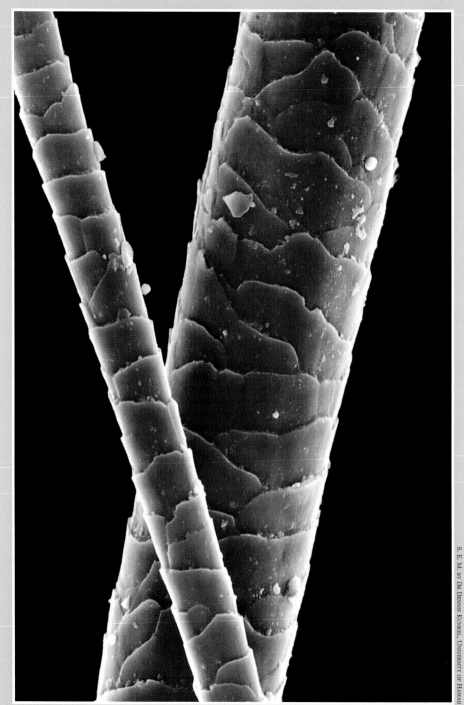

The hair of a German Shepherd Dog enlarged 1,200X. Note the broken ends of the hair wall. This is the origin of dandruff.

minimise tangles and mats, get rid of dust and dandruff, and remove any dead hair. Regular grooming sessions are also a good way to spend time with your dog. Many dogs grow to like the feel of being brushed and will enjoy the daily routine.

BATHING

Dogs do not need to be bathed as often as humans, but regular bathing is essential for healthy skin and a healthy, shiny coat. Again, like most anything, if you accustom your pup to being bathed as a puppy, it will be second nature by the time he grows up. You want your dog to be at ease in the bath or else it could end up a wet,

soapy, messy ordeal for both of you!

Brush your German Shepherd thoroughly before wetting his coat. This will get rid of most mats and tangles, which are harder to remove when the coat is wet. Make that your dog has a good non-slip surface to

By making brushing a normal routine, your German Shepherd Dog will grow to enjoy the experience.

stand on. Begin by wetting the dog's coat. A shower or hose attachment is necessary for thoroughly wetting and rinsing the coat. Check the water temperature to make sure that it is neither too hot nor too cold.

Next, apply shampoo to the dog's coat and work it into a good lather. You should purchase a shampoo that is made for dogs; do not use a product made for human hair. Washing the head last; you do not want shampoo to drip into the dog's eyes while you are washing the rest of his body. Work the shampoo all the way down to the skin. You can use this opportunity to check the skin for any bumps, bites or other abnormalities. Do not neglect

DID YOU KNOW?

How much grooming equipment you purchase will depend on how much grooming you are going to do. Here are some basics for the German Shepherd Dog:

- Natural bristle brush
- Slicker brush
- Metal comb
- Scissors
- Blaster
- Electric clippers
- Rubber mat
- Dog shampoo
- Spray hose attachment
- Ear cleaner
- Cotton wipes
- Heavy towels
- Nail clippers
- Wide-tooth metal rake

DID YOU KNOW?

The use of human soap products like shampoo, bubble bath and soap can be very deleterious to a German Shepherd Dog's coat and skin. Human products are too strong and remove the protective oils coating the dogs hair and skin (making him water resistant).

The only time a German Shepherd Dog needs a bath is when he gets a dirty coat or when the veterinary surgeon prescribes a medicated bath. In any case, only use shampoo made especially for dogs.

any area of the body—get all of the hard-to-reach places.

Once the dog has been thoroughly shampooed, he requires an equally thorough rinsing. Shampoo left in the coat can be irritating to the skin. Protect his eyes from the shampoo by shielding them with your hand and directing the

flow of water in the opposite direction. You should also avoid getting water in the ear canal. Be prepared for your dog to shake out his coat—you might want to stand back, but make sure you have a hold on the dog to keep him from running through the house.

DID YOU KNOW?

Once you are sure that the dog is thoroughly rinsed, squeeze the excess water out of the coat with your hand and dry him with a heavy towel. You may choose to blow-dry his coat or just let it dry naturally. In cold weather, never allow your dog outside with a wet coat.

There are 'dry bath' products on the market, which are sprays and powders intended for spot cleaning, that can be used between regular baths, if necessary. They are not substitutes for regular baths, but they are easy to use for touch-ups as they do not require rinsing.

EAR CLEANING

The ears should be kept clean and any excess hair inside the ear should be trimmed. Ears can be cleaned with a cotton wipe and special cleaner or ear powder made especially for dogs. Be on the lookout for any signs of infection or ear mite infestation. If your German Shepherd has been shaking his head or scratching at his ears frequently, this usually indicates a problem. If his ears have an unusual odour, this is a sure sign of mite infestation or infection, and

Use a cotton wipe to clean any debris from your Shepherd pup's ears. Inspect them for signs of mites, foul odours and possible irritation.

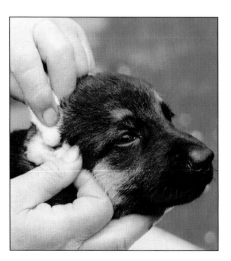

a signal to have his ears checked by the veterinary surgeon.

NAIL CLIPPING

Your German Shepherd should be accustomed to having his nails trimmed at an early age, since it will be part of your maintenance routine throughout his life. Not only does it look nicer, but a dog with long nails can cause injury if he jumps up or if he scratches someone unintentionally. Also, a long nail has a better chance of ripping and bleeding, or causing the feet to spread. A good rule of thumb is that if you can hear your dog's nails clicking on the floor when he walks, his nails are too long.

Before you start cutting, make sure you can identify the 'quick' in each nail. The quick is a blood vessel that runs through the centre of each nail and grows rather close to the end. It will bleed if accidentally cut, which will be quite painful for the dog as it contains nerve endings. Keep some type of clotting agent on hand, such as a styptic pencil or styptic powder (the type used for shaving). This will stop the bleeding quickly when applied to the end of the cut nail. Do not panic if this happens, just stop the bleeding and talk soothingly to your dog. Once he has calmed down, move on to the next nail. It is better to clip a little at a time, particularly with black-nailed dogs.

Hold your pup steady as you begin trimming his nails; you do not want him to make any sudden movements or run away. Talk to him soothingly and stroke his fur as you clip. Holding his

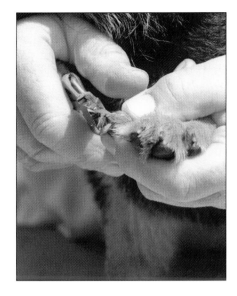

Cutting the nails is an art you should learn from your vet. The nails should not be cut too short or they will bleed.

foot in your hand, simply take off the end of each nail in one quick clip. You can purchase nail clippers that are specially made for dogs; you can probably find them wherever you buy pet or grooming supplies.

DID YOU KNOW?

A dog that spends a lot of time outside on a hard surface such as cement or pavement will have his nails naturally worn down and may not need to have them trimmed as often, except maybe in the colder months when he is not outside as much. Regardless, it is best to get your German Shepherd accustomed to this procedure at an early age so that he is used to it. Some dogs are especially sensitive about having their feet touched, but if a dog has experienced it since he was young, he should not be bothered by it.

61

BREED-SPECIFIC GROOMING CONSIDERATIONS

German Shepherds do not require fancy grooming or elaborate haircuts. Basically, the main goal in grooming the German Shepherd is to keep the dog's coat looking nice and in good health. German Shepherds do shed, so during shedding seasons you will need to pay more attention to his coat. A metal rake or comb will aid in removing mats from the undercoat. A vigorous brushing will loosen much of the dead hair. Follow up with a metal comb to remove the hair that is being shed.

Offer your German Shepherd water when travelling. Be sure to stop often to let him relieve himself.

> **DID YOU KNOW?**
>
> The most extensive travel you do with your dog may be limited to trips to the veterinary surgeon's office—or you may decide to bring him along for long distances when the family goes on holiday. Whichever the case, it is important to consider your dog's safety while travelling.

TRAVELLING WITH YOUR DOG

AUTOMOBILE TRAVEL

You should accustom your German Shepherd to riding in an auto at an early age. You may or may not often take him in the auto, but at the very least he will need to go to the vet and you do not want these trips to be traumatic for the dog or a big hassle for you. The safest way for a dog to ride in the auto is in his crate. If he uses a fibreglass crate in the house, you can use the same crate for travel. If you have a wire crate in the house, consider purchasing an appropriately sized fibreglass crate for travelling. Wire crates can be used for travel, but fibreglass

> **DID YOU KNOW?**
>
> A point that deserves mentioning is never leave your dog alone in the auto. In hot weather your dog can die from the high temperature inside a closed vehicle, and leaving the window open is dangerous as well since the dog can hurt himself trying to get out.

crates are safer.

Put the pup in the crate and see how he reacts. If he seems uneasy, you can have a passenger hold him on his lap while you drive. Another option is a specially made safety harness for dogs, which straps the dog in much like a seat belt. Do not let the dog roam loose in the vehicle—this is *very* dangerous! If you should stop short, your dog can be thrown and injured. If the dog starts climbing on you and pestering you while you are driving, you will not be able to concentrate on the road. It is an unsafe situation for everyone—human and canine.

For long trips, be prepared to stop to let the dog relieve himself. Bring along whatever you need to clean up after him. You should bring along some old towels and rags, should he have an accident in the auto or become carsick.

DID YOU KNOW?

For international travel you will have to make arrangements well in advance (perhaps months), as countries' regulations pertaining to bringing in animals differ. There may be special health certificates and/or vaccinations that your dog will need before taking the trip, sometimes this has to be done within a certain time frame. In rabies-free countries, you will need to bring proof of the dog's rabies vaccination and there may be a quarantine period upon arrival.

AIR TRAVEL

Whilst it is possible to take a dog on a flight within Britain, this is fairly unusual and advance permission is always required. You will have to contact the airline before travelling. The dog will be required to travel in a fibreglass crate; you may be able to use your

Sturdy fibreglass crates are needed for travelling.

own or the airline can usually supply one. To help the dog be at ease, put one of his favourite toys in the crate with him. Rules require that the dog has access to water, but do not feed him for at least six hours before the trip. Once the flight is underway, there will be nowhere to go to relieve himself, and you do not want him to be uncomfortable trying to hold it in so as not to soil the crate.

Make sure your dog is properly identified and that your contact infor-

Two dogs? Two crates. Dogs should not be allowed to roam freely in your auto.

Your German Shepherd Dog will probably be happier and safer in a proper kennel than travelling with you. You should find a suitable kennel in your neighbourhood so that your dog is in good hands when you travel.

mation appears on his ID tags and on his crate. Animals travel in a different area of the plane than human passengers, and, although transporting animals is routine for large airlines, there is always that slight risk of getting separated from your dog.

BOARDING

So you want to take a family holiday—and you want to include *all* members of the family. You would probably make arrangements for accommodations ahead of time anyway, but this is especially important when travelling with a dog. You do not want to make an overnight stop at the only place around for miles to find out that they do not allow dogs. Also, you do not want to reserve a place for your family without mentioning that you are bringing a dog, because if it is against their policy you may not have a place to stay.

Alternatively, if you are travelling and choose not to bring your German Shepherd, you will have to

DID YOU KNOW?

If your dog gets lost, he is not able to ask for directions home.

Identification tags fastened to the collar give important information— the dog's name, the owner's name, the owner's address and a telephone number where the owner can be reached. This makes it easy for whoever finds the dog to contact the owner and arrange to have the dog returned. An added advantage is that a person will be more likely to approach a lost dog who has ID tags on his collar; it tells the person that this is somebody's pet rather than a stray. This is the easiest and fastest method of identification provided that the tags stay on the collar and the collar stays on the dog.

make arrangements for him while you are away. Some options are to bring him to a neighbour's house to stay while you are gone, to have a trusted neighbour stop by often or stay at your house, or bring your dog to a reputable boarding kennel. If you choose to board him at a kennel, you should stop by to see the facility and where the dogs are kept to make sure that it is clean. Talk to some of the employees and see how they treat the dogs—do they spend time with the dogs, play with them, exercise them, etc.? You know that your German Shepherd will not be happy unless he gets regular activity. Also find out the kennel's policy on vaccinations and what they require. This is for all of the dogs' safety, since when dogs are kept together, there

is a greater risk of diseases being passed from dog to dog. Many veterinary surgeons offer boarding facilities; this is another option.

IDENTIFICATION

Your German Shepherd is your valued companion and friend. That is why you always keep a close eye on him and you have made sure that he cannot escape from the garden or wriggle out of his collar and run away from you. However, accidents can happen and there may come a time when your dog unexpectedly gets separated from you. If this unfortunate event should occur, the first thing on your mind will be finding him. Proper identification will increase the chances of his being returned to you safely and quickly.

Your German Shepherd Dog should have a stout collar with proper identification tags attached thereto.

Your German Shepherd is your valued friend—take precautions to keep him safe.

The German Shepherd Dog's working ability and trainability have earned him the distinction of being the most recognisable service dog in the world. This guide dog is being trained at the Seeing Eye® facility.

Housebreaking and Training Your German Shepherd Dog

Living with an untrained dog is a lot like owning a piano that you do not know how to play—it is a nice object to look at but it does not do much more than that to bring you pleasure. Now try taking piano lessons and suddenly the piano comes alive and brings forth magical sounds and rhythms that set your heart singing and your body swaying.

The same is true with your German Shepherd. At first you enjoy seeing him around the house. He does not do much with you other than to need food, water and exercise. Come to think of it, he does not bring you much joy, either. He is a big responsibility with a very small return. And often, he develops unacceptable behaviours that annoy and/or infuriate you to say nothing of bad habits that may end up costing you great sums of money. Not a good thing!

Now train your German Shepherd. Enroll in an obedience class. Teach him good manners as you learn how and why he behaves the way he does. Find out how to communicate with your dog and how to recognise and understand his communications with you. Suddenly the dog takes on a new role in your life—he is smart, interesting, well behaved and fun to be with, and he demonstrates his

bond of devotion to you daily. In other words, your German Shepherd does wonders for your ego because he constantly reminds you that you are not only his leader, you are his hero! Miraculous things have happened—you have a wonderful dog (even your family and friends have noticed the transformation!) and you feel good about yourself.

Those involved with teaching dog obedience and counselling owners

Training is necessary to ensure that your German Shepherd Dog grows up to be polite and well behaved.

about their dogs' behaviour have discovered some interesting facts about dog ownership. For example, training dogs when they are puppies results in the highest rate of success in develop-

German Shepherd Dogs are more trainable as puppies.

ing well-mannered and well-adjusted adult dogs. Training an older dog, say from six months to six years of age, can produce almost equal results providing that the owner accepts the dog's slower rate of learning capability and is willing to work patiently to help the dog succeed at developing to his fullest potential. Unfortunately,

the patience factor is what many owners of untrained adult dogs lack, so they do not persist until their dogs are successful at learning particular behaviours.

Training a puppy, for example, aged 8 to 16 weeks (20 weeks at the most) is like working with a dry sponge in a pool of water. The pup soaks up whatever you show him and constantly looks for more things to do and learn. At this early age, his body is not yet producing hormones, and therein lies the reason for such a high rate of success. Without hormones, he is focused on his owners and not particularly interested in investigating other places, dogs, people, etc. You are his leader; his provider of food, water, shelter and security. Therefore, he latches onto you and wants to stay close. He will usually follow you from room to room, will not let you out of his sight when you are outdoors with

Dogs are pack animals. There can only be one leader. Make sure it is you— not your German Shepherd or another dog!

Dogs leave their tongues out to control body temperature. The saliva evaporates, thus cooling the blood in the dog's tongue.

him, and respond in like manner to the people and animals you encounter. If, for example, you greet a friend warmly, he will be happy to greet the person as well. If, however, you are hesitant, even anxious, about the approach of a stranger, he will respond accordingly.

Once the puppy begins to produce hormones, his natural curiosity emerges and he begins to investigate the world around him. It is at that time when you may notice that the untrained dog begins to wander away from you and even ignore your commands to stay close. When this behaviour becomes a problem, the owner has two choices: get rid of the dog or train him. It is strongly urged that you choose the latter option.

Occasionally there are no classes available within a reasonable distance from the owner's home. Sometimes

DID YOU KNOW?

If you have other pets in the home and/or interact often with the pets of friends and other family members, your pup will respond to those pets in much the same manner as you do. It is only when you show fear or resentment toward another animal that he will act fearful or unfriendly.

there are classes available but the tuition is too costly. Whatever the circumstances, the solution to the problem of lack of lesson availability lies within the pages of this book.

This chapter is devoted to helping you train your German Shepherd at home. If the recommended procedures are followed faithfully, you may expect positive results that will prove

No dog, whether adult or puppy, likes shouting, pain or solitude. A German Shepherd puppy can be trained to be your best friend...the secret is the word 'trained.'

rewarding to both you and your dog.

Whether your German Shepherd is a puppy or a mature adult, the methods of teaching and the techniques we use in training basic behaviours are the same. After all, no dog, whether puppy or adult, likes harsh or inhumane methods. All creatures, however, respond favourably to gentle motivational methods and sincere praise and encouragement. Now let us get started.

HOUSEBREAKING

You can train a puppy to relieve itself wherever you choose. For example, city dwellers often train their puppies to relieve themselves in the gutter because large plots of grass are not readily available. Suburbanites, on the other hand, usually have gardens to accommodate their dogs' needs.

Outdoor training includes such surfaces as grass, dirt and cement. Indoor training usually means training your dog to newspaper.

When deciding on the surface and location that you will want your German Shepherd to use, be sure it is going to be permanent. Training your dog to grass and then changing your mind two months later is extremely difficult for both dog and owner.

Next, choose the command you will use each and every time you want your puppy to void. 'Go hurry up' and 'Go make' are examples of commands commonly used by dog owners.

Get in the habit of asking the puppy, 'Do you want to go hurry up?' (or whatever your chosen relief command is) before you take him out. That way, when he becomes an adult, you will be able to determine if he wants to go out when you ask him. A confirmation will be signs of interest, wagging his tail, watching you intently, going to the door, etc.

70

Canine Development Schedule

It is important to understand how and at what age a puppy develops into adulthood. If you are a puppy owner, consult the following Canine Development Schedule to determine the stage of development your German Shepherd puppy is currently experiencing. This knowledge will help you as you work with the puppy in the weeks and months ahead.

Period	Age	Characteristics
FIRST TO THIRD	**BIRTH TO SEVEN WEEKS**	Puppy needs food, sleep and warmth, and responds to simple and gentle touching. Needs mother for security and disciplining. Needs litter mates for learning and interacting with other dogs. Pup learns to function within a pack and learns pack order of dominance. Begin socialising with adults and children for short periods. Begins to become aware of its environment.
FOURTH	**EIGHT TO TWELVE WEEKS**	Brain is fully developed. Needs socialising with outside world. Remove from mother and littermates. Needs to change from canine pack to human pack. Human dominance necessary. Fear period occurs between 8 and 16 weeks. Avoid fright and pain.
FIFTH	**THIRTEEN TO SIXTEEN WEEKS**	Training and formal obedience should begin. Less association with other dogs, more with people, places, situations. Period will pass easily if you remember this is pup's change-to-adolescence time. Be firm and fair. Flight instinct prominent. Permissiveness and over-disciplining can do permanent damage. Praise for good behaviour.
JUVENILE	**FOUR TO EIGHT MONTHS**	Another fear period about 7 to 8 months of age. It passes quickly, but be cautious of fright and pain. Sexual maturity reached. Dominant traits established. Dog should understand sit, down, come and stay by now.

NOTE: THESE ARE APPROXIMATE TIME FRAMES. ALLOW FOR INDIVIDUAL DIFFERENCES IN PUPPIES.

Your German Shepherd puppy will find a favourite spot in which to relieve himself. Be sure that spot is convenient for you so that you can take him there when necessary.

PUPPY'S NEEDS

Puppy needs to relieve himself after play periods, after each meal, after he has been sleeping and any time he indicates that he is looking for a place to urinate or defecate.

The urinary and intestinal tract muscles of very young puppies are not fully developed. Therefore, like human babies, puppies need to relieve themselves frequently.

Take your puppy out often—every hour for an eight-week-old, for example. The older the puppy, the less often he will need to relieve him-

self. Finally, as a mature healthy adult, he will require only three to five relief trips per day.

HOUSING

Since the types of housing and control you provide for your puppy has a direct relationship on the success of house-training, we consider the various aspects of both before we begin training.

The only reliable housebreaking success results from consistency in training.

> ### DID YOU KNOW?
> Success that comes by luck is usually happenstance and frequently short lived. Success that comes by well-thought-out proven methods is often more easily achieved and permanent. This is the Success Method. It is designed to give you, the puppy owner, a simple yet proven way to help your German Shepherd puppy develop clean living habits and a feeling of security in his new environment.

Bringing a new puppy home and turning him loose in your house can be compared to turning a child loose in a sports arena and telling the child that the place is all his! The sheer enormity of the place would be too much for him to handle.

Instead, offer the puppy clearly defined areas where he can play, sleep, eat and live. A room of the house where the family gathers is the most obvious choice. Puppies are social animals and need to feel a part of the pack right from the start. Hearing your voice, watching you while

ideal for providing safety and security for both puppy and owner.

Within that room there should be a smaller area which the puppy can call his own. A cubbyhole, a wire or fibreglass dog crate or a fenced (not boarded!) corner from which he can

Puppies need to relieve them-selves frequently.

view the activities of his new family will be fine. The size of the area or crate is the key factor here. The area must be large enough for the puppy to lay down and stretch out as well as stand up without rubbing his head on the top, yet small enough so that he cannot relieve himself at one end and sleep at the other without coming into contact with his droppings.

Dogs are, by nature, clean animals and will not remain close to their relief areas unless forced to do so. In those cases, they then become dirty dogs and usually remain that way for life.

The crate or cubby should be lined with a clean towel and offer one toy, no more. Do not put food or water in the crate, as eating and drinking will activate his digestive processes and ultimately defeat your purpose as well as make the puppy very uncomfortable as he attempts to 'hold it.'

DID YOU KNOW?

Most of all, be consistent. Always take your dog to the same location, always use the same command, and always have him on lead when he is in his relief area, unless a fenced-in garden is available.

By following the Success Method, your German Shepherd puppy will be completely housetrained by the time his muscle and brain development reach maturity. Keep in mind that small breeds usually mature faster than large breeds, even though large breeds like the German Shepherd grow rapidly, but all puppies should be trained by six months of age.

---

you are doing things and smelling you nearby are all positive reinforcers that he is now a member of your pack. Usually a family room, the kitchen or a nearby adjoining breakfast nook is

Recognise the signs— this German Shepherd Dog is staring at his favourite relief area, hoping somebody will let him out! Some dogs always seem to be on the wrong side of the door.

If the puppy chews on the arm of the chair when he is alone, you will probably discipline him angrily when you get home. Thus, he makes the association that your coming home means he is going to be hit or punished. (He will not remember chewing up the chair and is incapable of making the association of the discipline with his naughty deed.)

Other times of excitement, such as family parties, etc., can be fun for the puppy providing he can view the activities from the security of his crate. He is not underfoot and he

CONTROL

By control, we mean helping the puppy to create a lifestyle pattern that will be compatible to that of his human pack (YOU!). Just as we guide little children to learn our way of life, we must show the puppy when it is time to play, eat, sleep, exercise and even entertain himself.

Your puppy should always sleep in his crate. He should also learn that, during times of household confusion and excessive human activity such as at breakfast when family members are preparing for the day, he can play by himself in relative safety and comfort in his crate. Each time you leave the puppy alone, he should be crated. Puppies are chewers. They cannot tell the difference between lamp cords, television wires, shoes, table legs, etc. Chewing into a television wire, for example, can be fatal to the puppy while a shorted wire can start a fire in the house.

DID YOU KNOW?

By providing sleeping and resting quarters that fit the dog, and offering frequent opportunities to relieve himself outside his quarters, the puppy quickly learns that the outdoors (or the newspaper if you are training him to paper) is the place to go when he needs to urinate or defecate. It also reinforces his innate desire to keep his sleeping quarters clean. This, in turn, helps develop the muscle control that will eventually produce a dog with clean living habits.

is not being fed all sorts of tidbits that will probably cause him stomach distress, yet he still feels a part of the fun.

SCHEDULE

As stated earlier, a puppy should be taken to his relief area each time he is released from his crate, after meals, after a play session, when he first awakens in the morning (at age 8 weeks, this can mean 5 a.m.!) and whenever he indicates by circling or sniffing busily that he needs to urinate or defecate. For a puppy less than ten weeks of age, a routine of taking him

> ### DID YOU KNOW?
> Never line your pup's sleeping area with newspaper. Puppy litters are usually raised on newspaper and, once in your home, the puppy will immediately associate newspaper with voiding. Never put newspaper on any floor while housetraining, as this will only confuse the puppy. If you are paper-training him, use paper in his designated relief area ONLY. Finally, restrict water intake after evening meals. Offer a few licks at a time—never let a young puppy gulp water after meals.

out every hour is necessary. As the puppy grows, he will be able to wait for longer periods of time.

Keep trips to his relief area short. Stay no more than five or six minutes and then return to the house. If he goes during that time, praise him lavishly and take him indoors immediately. If he does not, but he has an accident when you go back indoors, pick him up immediately, say 'No! No!' and return to his relief area. Wait a few minutes, then return to the house again. NEVER hit a puppy or rub his

face in urine or excrement when he has an accident!

Once indoors, put the puppy in his crate until you have had time to clean up his accident. Then release him to the family area and watch him more closely than before. Chances are, his accident was a result of your not picking up his signal or waiting too long before offering him the opportunity to relieve himself. NEVER hold a grudge against the puppy for accidents.

Let the puppy learn that going

Clean up after your dog.

outdoors means it is time to relieve himself, not play. Once trained, he will be able to play indoors and out and still differentiate between the times for play versus the times for relief.

Help him develop regular hours for naps, being alone, playing by himself and just resting, all in his crate.

> ### DID YOU KNOW?
> If you have a small child in the home who wants to get into the puppy's food bowl every time he eats, feeding the pup in his crate is the answer. The child cannot disturb the dog and the pup will be free to eat in peace.

75

Male dogs leave territorial markers via their urination.

A dog may start his excretory ritual by pulling his back legs forward. Do not interrupt him at this stage.

Encourage him to entertain himself while you are busy with your activities. Let him learn that having you near is comforting, but it is not your main purpose in life to provide him with undivided attention.

Each time you put a puppy in his crate tell him, 'Crate time!' (or whatever command you choose). Soon, he will run to his crate when he hears you say those words.

In the beginning of his training, do not leave him in his crate for prolonged periods of time except during the night when everyone is sleeping. Make his experience with his crate a pleasant one and, as an adult, he will love his crate and willingly stay in it for several hours. There are millions

of people who go to work every day and leave their adult dogs crated while they are away. The dogs accept this as their lifestyle and look forward to 'crate time.'

Crate training provides safety for you, the puppy and the home. It also provides the puppy with a feeling of security, and that helps the puppy achieve self-confidence and clean habits.

Remember that one of the primary ingredients in housetraining your puppy is control. Regardless of your

lifestyle, there will always be occasions when you will need to have a place where your dog can stay and be happy and safe. Crate training is the answer for now and in the future.

In conclusion, a few key elements are really all you need for a successful house and crate training method—consistency, frequency, praise, control and supervision. By following these procedures with a normal, healthy puppy, you and the puppy will soon

Once trained, your German Shepherd Dog will know when it is 'bathroom time' and will go to his spot in the yard without your guidance.

be past the stage of 'accidents' and ready to move on to a full and rewarding life together.

ROLES OF DISCIPLINE, REWARD AND PUNISHMENT

Discipline, training one to act in accordance with rules, brings order to life. It is as simple as that. Without discipline, particularly in a group society, chaos reigns supreme and the group will eventually perish. Humans and canines are social animals and need some form of discipline in order to function effectively. They must procure food, protect their home base

Crate training is wonderful. Your German Shepherd's crate should be large enough that he is comfortable in it. A crate that is too small will seem like a prison rather than a den.

THE SUCCESS METHOD
6 Steps to Successful Crate Training

1 Tell the puppy 'Crate time!' and place him in the crate with a small treat (a piece of cheese or half of a biscuit). Let him stay in the crate for five minutes while you are in the same room. Then release him and praise lavishly. Never release him when he is fussing. Wait until he is quiet before you let him out.

2 Repeat Step 1 several times a day.

3 The next day, place the puppy in the crate as before. Let him stay there for ten minutes. Do this several times.

4 Continue building time in five-minute increments until the puppy stays in his crate for 30 minutes with you in the room. Always take him to his relief area after prolonged periods in his crate.

5 Now go back to Step 1 and let the puppy stay in his crate for five minutes, this time while you are out of the room.

6 Once again, build crate time in five-minute increments with you out of the room. When the puppy will stay willingly in his crate (he may even fall asleep!) for 30 minutes with you out of the room, he will be ready to stay in it for several hours at a time.

A trained dog is a pet; an untrained dog is an animal.

and their young and reproduce to keep the species going.

If there were no discipline in the lives of social animals, they would eventually die from starvation and/or predation by other stronger animals.

In the case of domestic canines, dogs need discipline in their lives in order to understand how their pack (you and other family members) function and how they must act in order to survive.

A large humane society in a highly populated area recently surveyed dog owners regarding their satisfaction with their relationships with their dogs. People who had trained their dogs were 75% more satisfied with their pets than those who had never trained their dogs.

Dr. Edward Thorndike, a psychologist, established *Thorndike's Theory of Learning*, which states that a behaviour that results in a pleasant event tends to be repeated. A behaviour that results in an unpleasant event tends not to be repeated. It is this theory on which training methods are based today. For example, if you manipulate a dog to perform a specific behaviour and reward him for doing it, he is likely to do it again because he enjoyed the end result.

Occasionally, punishment, a penalty inflicted for an offence, is necessary. The best type of punishment often comes from an outside source. For example, a child is told not to touch the stove because he may get burned. He disobeys and touches the stove. In doing so, he receives a burn. From that time on, he respects the heat of the stove and avoids contact with it. Therefore, a behaviour that results in an unpleasant event tends not to be repeated.

DID YOU KNOW?

The puppy should also have regular play and exercise sessions when he is with you or a family member. Exercise for a very young puppy can consist of a short walk around the house or garden. Playing can include fetching games with a large ball or an old sock with a knot tied in the middle. (All puppies teethe and need soft things upon which to chew.) Remember to restrict play periods to indoors within his living area (the family room for example) until he is completely housetrained.

DID YOU KNOW?

Practice Makes Perfect!
• Have training lessons with your dog every day in several short segments—three to five times a day for a few minutes at a time is ideal.
• Do not have long practice sessions. The dog will become easily bored.
• Never practice when you are tired, ill, worried or in an otherwise negative mood. This will transmit to the dog and may have an adverse effect on its performance.
   Think fun, short and above all POSITIVE! End each session on a high note, rather than a failed exercise, and make sure to give a lot of praise. Enjoy the training and help your dog enjoy it, too.

A good example of a dog learning the hard way is the dog who chases the house cat. He is told many times to leave the cat alone, yet he persists in teasing the cat. Then, one day he begins chasing the cat but the cat turns and swipes a claw across the dog's face, leaving him with a painful gash on his nose. The final result is that the dog stops chasing the cat.

TRAINING EQUIPMENT

COLLAR

A simple buckle collar is fine for most dogs. One who pulls mightily on the leash may require a chain choker collar. Only in the most severe cases of a dog being totally out of control is it recommended to use a prong or pinch collar, and in this case only if the owner has been instructed in the proper use of such equipment.

LEAD

A 1- to 2-metre lead is recommended, preferably made of leather, nylon or heavy cloth. A chain lead is not recommended, as many dog owners find that the chain cuts into their hands and that switching the lead back and forth frequently between their hands is painful.

TREATS

Have a bag of treats on hand. Something nutritious and easy to swallow works best; use a soft treat, a chunk of cheese or a piece of cooked chicken rather than a dry biscuit. By the time the dog gets done chewing a dry treat, he will forget why he is being rewarded in the first place! Using food rewards will not teach a dog to beg at the table—the only way to teach a dog

Training requires trust and commitment.

to beg at the table is to give him food from the table. In training, rewarding the dog with a food treat away from the table will help him associate praise and the treats with learning new behaviours that obviously please his owner.

Working and service dogs wear special harnesses when performing their duties. These leather harnesses are worn by German Shepherds that work as guide dogs.

Try on the collar, harness and/or lead to be sure it is comfortable for both you and the dog.

TRAINING BEGINS: ASK THE DOG A QUESTION

In order to teach your dog anything, you must first get his attention. After all, he cannot learn anything if he is looking away from you with his mind on something else.

To get his attention, ask him, 'School?' and immediately walk over to him and give him a treat as you tell him 'Good dog.' Wait a minute or two and repeat the routine, this time with a treat in your hand as you approach the dog to within a foot of him. Do not go directly to him, but stop about a foot short of him and hold out the treat as you ask, 'School?' He will see you approaching with a treat in your hand and most likely begin walking toward you. As you meet, give him the treat and praise again.

The third time, ask the question, have a treat in your hand and walk only a short distance toward the dog so that he must walk almost all the way to you. As he reaches you, give him the treat and praise again.

By this time, the dog will probably

be getting the idea that if he pays attention to you, especially when you ask that question, it will pay off in treats and fun activities for him. In other words, he learns that 'school' means doing fun things with you that result in treats and positive attention for him.

Remember that the dog does not understand your verbal language, he only recognises sounds. Your question translates to a series of sounds for him, and those sounds become the signal to go to you and pay attention; if he does, he will get to interact with you plus receive treats and praise.

THE BASIC COMMANDS

TEACHING SIT

Now that you have the dog's attention, hold the lead in your left hand and the food treat in your right. Place your food hand at the dog's nose and let him lick the treat but not take it from you. Say 'Sit' and slowly raise your food hand from in front of the dog's nose up over his head so that he is looking at the ceiling. As he bends his head upward, he will have to bend his knees to maintain his balance. As he bends his knees, he will assume a sit position. At that point, release the food treat and praise lavishly with comments such as 'Good dog! Good sit!', etc. Remember to always praise enthusiastically, because dogs relish verbal praise from their owners and feel so proud of themselves whenever they accomplish a behaviour.

You will not use food forever in getting the dog to obey your commands. Food is only used to teach new behaviours, and once the dog knows what you want when you give a specific command, you will wean him off of the food treats but still maintain the verbal praise. After all, you will always have your voice with you, but there will be many times when you have no food rewards yet you expect the dog to obey.

TEACHING DOWN

Teaching the down exercise is easy when you understand how the dog perceives the down position, and it is very difficult when you do not. In addition, teaching the down exercise using the wrong method can sometimes make the dog develop such a fear of the down that he either runs away when you say 'down' or he attempts to bite the person who tries to force him down.

Have the dog sit close alongside your left leg, facing in the same direction as you are. Hold the lead in your left hand and a food treat in your right. Now place your left hand lightly on the top of the dog's shoulders where they meet above the spinal cord. Do not push down on

Sit is one of the first commands you will teach your German Shepherd Dog.

You may have to help your German Shepherd into the sit position until he is used to it.

When the dog's elbows touch the floor, release the food and praise softly. Try to get the dog to maintain that down position for several seconds before you let him sit up again. The goal here is to get the dog to settle down and not feel threatened in the down position.

TEACHING STAY

It is easy to teach the dog to stay in either a sit or a down position. Again, we use food and praise during the teaching process as we help the dog to understand exactly what it is that we are expecting him to do.

To teach the sit/stay, start with the dog sitting on your left side as before and hold the lead in your left hand. Have a food treat in your right hand and place your food hand at the dog's nose. Say 'Stay' and step out on your right foot to stand directly in front of the dog, toe to toe, as he licks and nibbles the treat. Be sure to keep his head facing upward to maintain the sit position. Count to five and then swing around to stand next to the dog again

the dog's shoulders; simply rest your left hand there so you can guide the dog to lie down close to your left leg rather than to swing away from your side when he drops.

Now place the food hand at the dog's nose, say 'Down' very softly (almost a whisper), and slowly lower the food hand to the dog's front feet. When the food hand reaches the floor, begin moving it forward along the floor in front of the dog. Keep talking softly to the dog, saying things like, 'Do you want this treat? You can do this, good dog.' Your reassuring tone of voice will help calm the dog as he tries to follow the food hand in order to get the treat.

> **DID YOU KNOW?**
> A dog in jeopardy never lies down. He stays alert on his feet because instinct tells him that he may have to run away or fight for his survival. Therefore, if a dog feels threatened or anxious, he will not lie down. Consequently, it is important to have the dog calm and relaxed as he learns the down exercise.

with him on your left. As soon as you get back to the original position, release the food and praise lavishly.

To teach the down/stay, do the down as previously described. As soon as the dog lies down, say 'Stay' and step out on your right foot just as you did in the sit/stay. Count to five and then return to stand beside the dog with him on your left side. Release the treat and praise as always.

Within a week or ten days, you can begin to add a bit of distance between you and your dog when you leave him. When you do, use your left hand open with the palm facing the dog as a stay signal, much the same as the hand signal a police officer uses to stop traffic at an intersection. Hold the food treat in your right hand as before, but this time the food is not touching the dog's nose. He will watch the food hand and quickly learn that he is going to get that treat as soon as you return to his side.

When you can stand 1 metre away from your dog for 30 seconds, you can then begin building time and distance in both stays. Eventually, the dog can be expected to remain in

DID YOU KNOW?

Dogs do not understand our language. They can be trained to react to a certain sound, at a certain volume. If you say 'No, Oliver' in a very soft pleasant voice it will not have the same meaning as 'No, Oliver!!' when you shout it as loud as you can. You should never use the dog's name during a reprimand, just the command NO!! Since dogs don't understand words, comics use dogs trained with opposite meanings to the world. Thus, when the comic commands his dog to SIT the dog will stand up; and vice versa.

the stay position for prolonged periods of time until you return to him or call him to you. Always praise lavishly when he stays.

TEACHING COME

If you make teaching 'Come' a fun experience, you should never have a 'student' that does not love the game or that fails to come when called. The secret, it seems, is never to teach the word 'Come.'

At times when an owner most wants his dog to come when called, the owner is likely upset or anxious and he allows these feelings to come through in the tone of his voice when he calls his dog. Hearing that desperation in his owner's voice, the dog fears the results of going to him and therefore either disobeys outright or runs in the opposite direction. The

You should be able to tell your German Shepherd Dog down and have him obey you instantly. Dogs should be taught this exercise when they are very young.

83

secret, therefore, is to teach the dog a game and, when you want him to come to you, simply play the game. It is practically a no-fail solution!

To begin, have several members of your family take a few food treats

Runaway dogs must come when called.

and each go into a different room in the house. Take turns calling the dog, and each person should celebrate the dog's finding him with a treat and lots of happy praise. When a person calls the dog, he is actually inviting the dog to find him and get a treat as a reward for 'winning.'

If the dog is tired and doesn't want to play (learn) any more, don't force him. Training should be fun for both of you. A few turns of the 'Where are you?' game and the dog will figure out that everyone is playing the game and that each person has a big celebration awaiting his success at locating them. Once he learns to love the game, simply calling out 'Where are you?' will bring him running from wherever he is when he hears that all-important question.

The come command is recognised as one of the most important things to teach a dog, so it is interesting to note that there are trainers who work with thousands of dogs and never teach the actual word 'Come.' Yet these dogs will race to respond to a person who uses the dog's name followed by

'Where are you?' In one instance, for example, a woman has a 12-year-old companion dog who went blind, but who never fails to locate her owner when asked, 'Where are you?'

Children particularly love to play this game with their dogs. Children can hide in smaller places like a shower stall or bathtub, behind a bed or under a table. The dog needs to work a little bit harder to find these hiding places, but when he does he loves to celebrate with a treat and a tussle with a favourite youngster.

TEACHING HEEL

Heeling means that the dog walks beside the owner without pulling. It takes time and patience on the owner's part to succeed at teaching the dog that he (the owner) will not proceed unless the dog is walking calmly beside him.

Pulling out ahead on the lead is definitely not acceptable.

Begin with holding the lead in your left hand as the dog sits beside your left leg. Hold the loop end of the lead in your right hand but keep your

DID YOU KNOW?

When calling the dog, do not say 'Come.' Say things like, 'Rover, where are you? See if you can find me! I have a cookie for you!' Keep up a constant line of chatter with coaxing sounds and frequent questions such as, 'Where are you?' The dog will learn to follow the sound of your voice to locate you and receive his reward.

left hand short on the lead so it keeps the dog in close next to you.

Say 'Heel' and step forward on your left foot. Keep the dog close to you and take three steps. Stop and have the dog sit next to you in what we now call the 'heel position.' Praise verbally, but do not touch the dog. Hesitate a moment and begin again with 'Heel,' taking three steps and stopping, at which point the dog is told to sit again.

Your goal here is to have the dog walk those three steps without pulling on the lead. When he will walk calmly beside you for three steps without pulling, increase the number of steps you take to five. When he will walk politely beside you while you take five steps, you can increase the length of your walk to ten steps. Keep increasing the length of your stroll until the dog will walk quietly beside you without pulling as long as you want him to heel. When you stop heeling, indicate to the dog that the exercise is over by verbally praising as you pet him and say 'OK, good

dog.' The 'OK' is used as a release word meaning that the exercise is finished and the dog is free to relax.

If you are dealing with a dog who insists on pulling you around, simply 'put on your brakes' and stand your ground until the dog realises that the two of you are not going anywhere until he is beside you and moving at your pace, not his. It may take some time just standing there to convince the dog that you are the leader and you will be the one to decide on the direction and speed of your travel.

Each time the dog looks up at you or slows down to give a slack lead

The ultimate training for a German Shepherd Dog is as a guide for the blind.

between the two of you, quietly praise him and say, 'Good heel. Good dog.' Eventually, the dog will begin to respond and within a few days he will be walking politely beside you without pulling on the lead. At first, the training sessions should be kept short and very positive; soon the dog will be able to walk nicely with you for increasingly longer distances. Remember also

Heel and sit are necessary commands.

to give the dog free time and the opportunity to run and play when you are done with heel practice.

WEANING OFF FOOD IN TRAINING

Food is used in training new behaviours, yet once the dog understands what behaviour goes with a specific command, it is time to start weaning him off the food treats. At first, give a treat after each exercise. Then, start to give a treat only after every other exercise. Mix up the times when you offer a food reward and the times when you only offer praise so that the dog will never know when he is going to receive both food and praise and when he is going to receive only praise. This is called a variable ratio reward system and it proves successful because

> **DID YOU KNOW?**
> If you begin teaching the heel by taking long walks and letting the dog pull you along, he misinterprets this action as an acceptable form of taking a walk. When you pull back on the lead to counteract his pulling, he reads that tug as a signal to pull even harder!

there is always the chance that the owner will produce a treat, so the dog never stops trying for that reward. No matter what, ALWAYS give verbal praise.

OBEDIENCE CLASSES

As previously discussed, it is a good idea to enroll in an obedience class if one is available in your area. Many areas have dog clubs that offer basic obedience training as well as preparatory classes for obedience competition. There are also local dog trainers who offer similar classes.

At obedience trials, dogs can earn titles at various levels of competition. The beginning levels of competition include basic behaviours such as sit, down, heel, etc. The more advanced levels of competition include jumping, retrieving, scent discrimination and signal work. The advanced levels require a dog and owner to put a lot of time and effort into their training; the titles that can be earned at these levels of competition are very prestigious.

OTHER ACTIVITIES FOR LIFE

Whether a dog is trained in the structured environment of a class or alone with his owner at home, there are many activities that can bring fun and rewards to both owner and dog once they have mastered basic control.

Teaching the dog to help out around the home, in the garden or on the farm provides great satisfaction to both dog and owner. In addition, the dog's help makes life a little easier for his owner and raises his stature as a valued companion to his family. It helps give the dog a purpose; it helps to keep his mind occupied and provides an outlet for his energy.

DID YOU KNOW?

Occasionally, a dog and owner who have not attended formal classes have been able to earn entry-level titles by obtaining competition rules and regulations from a local kennel club and practising on their own to a degree of perfection. Obtaining the higher level titles, however, almost always requires extensive training under the tutelage of experienced instructors. In addition, the more difficult levels require more specialised equipment whereas the lower levels do not.

Backpacking is an exciting and healthful activity that the dog can be taught without assistance from

All work and no play... These well-trained police dogs demonstrate how obedient and intelligent the German Shepherd can be. This display took place at the Crufts Dog Show.

more than his owner. The exercise of walking and climbing is good for man and dog alike, and the bond that they develop together is priceless.

If you are interested in participating in organised competition with your German Shepherd, there

Obedience competition is based on an owner guiding his/her dog through a series of obstacles and exercises.

are other activities other than obedience in which you and your dog can become involved. Agility is a popular and fun sport where dogs run through an obstacle course that includes various jumps, tunnels and other exercises to test the dog's speed and coordination. The owners often run through the course beside their dogs to give commands and to guide them through the course.

Although competitive, the focus is on fun—it's fun to do and fun to watch, as well as great exercise.

As a German Shepherd owner, you have the opportunity to participate in Schutzhund competition if you choose. Schutzhund originated as a test to determine the best quality German Shepherds to be used for breeding stock. It is now used as a way to evaluate working ability and temperament, and some German Shepherd owners choose to train and compete with their dogs in Schutzhund trials. There are three levels of Schutzhund, SchI, SchII and SchIII, each level being progressively more difficult to complete successfully. Each level consists of training, obedience and protection phases. Training for Schutzhund is intense and must be practised consistently to keep the dog keen. The experience of Schutzhund training is very rewarding for dog and owner, and the German Shepherd's tractability is well suited for this type of training.

A German Shepherd Dog that will not make eye contact will be difficult to train.

DID YOU KNOW?

If you start with a normal, healthy dog and give him time, patience and some carefully executed lessons, you will reap the rewards of that training for the life of the dog. And what a life it will be! The two of you will find immeasurable pleasure in the companionship you have built together with love, respect and understanding. Good luck and enjoy!

Your German Shepherd can be taught to retrieve upon command. You can even teach your dog to bring you the newspaper!

89

MEDICAL PROBLEMS MOST FREQUENTLY SEEN IN GERMAN SHEPHERDS

Condition	Age Affected	Cause	Area Affected
Acral Lick Dermatitis	Any age, males	Unknown	Legs
Aortic Stenosis	Young pups	Congenital	Heart
Cataracts	Less than 1 year	Congenital	Eye
Demodicosis	Less than 18 mos	Possibly congenital	Skin
Elbow Dysplasia	4 to 7 mos	Congenital	Elbow joint
Epilepsy	1 to 3 years	Congenital	Nervous system
Exocrine Pancreatic Insufficiency	Less than 2 years	Congenital	Pancreas
Gastric Dilatation (Bloat)	Older dogs	Swallowing air	Stomach
Hip Dysplasia	By 2 years	Congenital	Hip joint
Hypertrophic Osteodystrophy	3 to 4 mos	Organism or vitamin imbalance	Bones
Hypothyroidism	1 to 3 years	Lymphocytic thyroiditis	Endocrine system
Panosteitis	Less than 1 year, males	Unknown	Leg bones
Pannus	Any age	Possibly congenital	Cornea
Von Willebrand's Disease	Birth	Congenital	Blood

Health Care of German Shepherd Dogs

Dogs, being mammals like human beings, suffer many of the same physical illnesses as people. They might even share many of the psychological problems. Since people usually know more about human diseases than canine maladies, many of the terms used in this chapter will be the familiar terms, not necessarily those used by veterinary surgeons. We'll still use the term X-RAY, instead of the more acceptable term RADIOGRAPH. We will also use the familiar term SYMPTOMS even though dogs don't have symptoms, dogs have CLINICAL SIGNS. SYMPTOMS, by the way, are verbal descriptions of the patient's feelings. Since dogs can't speak, we have to look for clinical signs...but we still use the term SYMPTOMS in this book.

As a general rule, medicine is PRACTISED. That term is not arbi-

Your veterinary surgeon will be your dog's friend throughout his life.

trary. Medicine is an art. It is a constant changing art as we learn more and more about genetics, electronic aids (like CAT scans) and opinions. There are many dog maladies, like canine hip dysplasia, which are not universally treated in the same manner. Some veterinary surgeons opt for surgery more often than others.

SELECTING A VETERINARY SURGEON

Your selection of a veterinary surgeon should not be based upon personality (as most are) but upon their convenience to your home. You want a doctor who is close as you might have emergencies or multiple visits for treatments. You want a doctor who has services that you might require such as a boarding kennel, grooming facilities, who makes sophisticated pet supplies available and who has a

Veterinary surgeon examining an x-ray. You should befriend a vet before you buy your German Shepherd puppy.

good reputation for ability and responsiveness. There is nothing more frustrating than having to wait a day or more to get a response from a veterinary surgeon.

All veterinary surgeons are licensed and their diplomas and/or certificates should be displayed in their waiting rooms. There are, however, many veterinary specialties which usually require further studies and internships. There are specialists in heart problems (veterinary cardiologists), skin problems (veterinary dermatologists), teeth and gum problems (veterinary dentists), eye problems (veterinary ophthalmologists), X-rays (veterinary radiologists), and surgeons who have specialties in bones, muscles or other organs. Most veterinary surgeons do routine surgery such as neutering, stitching up wounds and docking tails for those breeds in which such is required for show purposes. When the problem affecting your dog is serious, it is not unusual or impudent to get another medical opinion. You might also want to compare costs between several veterinary surgeons. Sophisticated health care and veterinary services can be very costly. Don't be bashful to discuss these costs with your veterinary surgeon or his (her) staff. It is not infrequent that important decisions are based upon financial considerations.

PREVENTATIVE MEDICINE

It is much easier, less costly and more effective to practice preventative medicine than to fight bouts of illness and disease.

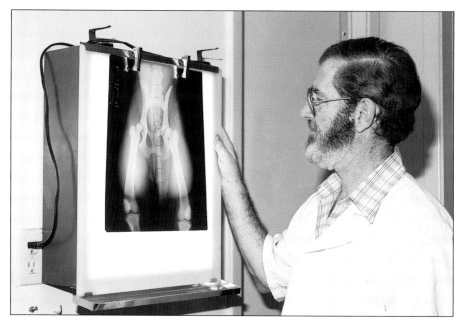

All veterinary surgeons are licensed and all have been taught to read x-rays, but there are specialists called veterinary radiologists who are consulted for the fine details of x-ray interpretation.

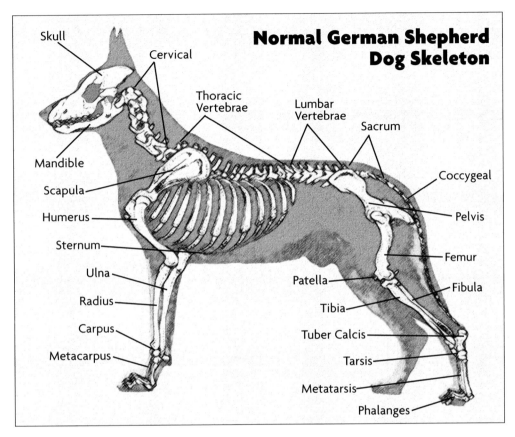

Normal German Shepherd Dog Skeleton

Skull
Cervical
Thoracic Vertebrae
Lumbar Vertebrae
Sacrum
Mandible
Scapula
Humerus
Sternum
Ulna
Radius
Carpus
Metacarpus
Coccygeal
Pelvis
Femur
Patella
Fibula
Tibia
Tuber Calcis
Tarsis
Metatarsis
Phalanges

Properly bred puppies come from parents that were selected based upon their genetic disease profile. Their mothers should have been vaccinated, free of all internal and external parasites, and properly nourished. For these reasons, a visit to the veterinary surgeon who cared for the dam (mother) is recommended. The dam can pass on disease resistance to her puppies. This resistance can last for 8-10 weeks. She can also pass on parasites and many infections. That's why you should visit the veterinary surgeon who cared for the dam.

AFTER WEANING TO FIVE MONTHS OLD

Puppies should be weaned by the time they are about two months old. A puppy that remains for at least eight weeks with its mother and litter mates usually adapts better to other dogs and people later in its life.

In every case, you should have your newly acquired puppy examined by a veterinary surgeon immediately. Vaccination programmes usually begin when the puppy is very young.

The puppy will have its teeth examined, have its skeletal conforma-

93

tion checked, and have its general health checked prior to certification by the veterinary surgeon. Many puppies have problems with their knee caps, eye cataracts and other eye problems, heart murmurs and undescended testicles. They may also have personality problems and your veterinary surgeon might have training in temperament evaluation. More puppies (dogs) are put to sleep because they behave poorly than all other medical conditions combined.

VACCINATION SCHEDULING

Most vaccinations are given by injection and should only be done by a veterinary surgeon. Both he and you should keep a record of the date of the injection, the identification of the vaccine and the amount given. Some vets give a first vaccination at eight weeks, but most breeders prefer not to commence until about 10 weeks because of negating any antibodies passed on by the dam. The vaccination schedule is usually based on a 15-day cycle. Take your vet's advice as to when to vaccinate. Most vaccinations immunise your puppy against viruses.

> **DID YOU KNOW?**
> Ridding your puppy of worms is VERY IMPORTANT because certain worms that puppies carry can infect humans, such as tapeworms, hookworms and roundworms.
>
> Since puppies are never housebroken at two to three weeks of age, it is easy for them to pass on the parasites (worms) to humans.
>
> Breeders initiate a deworming programme two weeks after weaning. The routine is repeated every two or three weeks until the puppy is three months old. The breeder from whom you obtained your German Shepherd puppy should provide you with the complete details of the deworming programme.
>
> Your veterinary surgeon can prescribe and monitor the programme of deworming for you. The usual programme is treating the puppy every 15-20 days until the puppy is positively worm free.
>
> It is not advised that you treat your puppy with drugs which are not recommended professionally.

Vaccinations are extremely important as infectious diseases can easily be passed from dog to dog.

The usual vaccines contain immunising doses of several different viruses such as distemper, parvovirus, parainfluenza and hepatitis. There are other vaccines available when the puppy is at risk. You should rely upon professional advice. This is especially true for the booster shot programme. Most vaccination programmes require a booster

HEALTH AND VACCINATION SCHEDULE

Age in Weeks:	3rd	6th	8th	10th	12th	14th	16th	20-24th
Worm Control	✔	✔	✔	✔	✔	✔	✔	✔
Neutering								✔
Heartworm*		✔						✔
Parvovirus		✔		✔		✔		✔
Distemper			✔		✔		✔	
Hepatitis			✔		✔		✔	
Leptospirosis		✔		✔		✔		
Parainfluenza		✔		✔		✔		
Dental Examination			✔					✔
Complete Physical			✔					✔
Temperament Testing			✔					
Coronavirus					✔			
Canine Cough		✔						
Hip Dysplasia							✔	
Rabies*								✔

Vaccinations are not instantly effective. It takes about two weeks for the dog's immunisation system to develop antibodies. Most vaccinations require annual booster shots. Your veterinary surgeon should guide you in this regard.
*Not applicable in the United Kingdom

when the puppy is a year old, and once a year thereafter. In some cases, circumstances may require more frequent immunisations.

Canine cough, more formally known as *tracheobronchitis*, is treated with a vaccine which is sprayed into the dog's nostrils.

The effectiveness of a parvovirus vaccination programme can be tested to be certain that the vaccinations are protective. Your veterinary surgeon will explain and manage all of these details.

FIVE MONTHS TO ONE YEAR OF AGE

By the time your puppy is five months old, he should have complet-

DID YOU KNOW?

Caring for the puppy starts before the puppy is born by keeping the dam healthy and well-nourished. When the puppy is about three weeks old, it must start its disease-control regimen. The first treatments will be for worms. Most puppies have worms, even if they are tested negative for worms. The test essentially is checking the stool specimens for the eggs of the worms. The worms continually shed eggs except during their dormant stage when they just rest in the tissues of the puppy. During this stage they don't shed eggs and are not evident during a routine examination.

95

ed his vaccination programme. During his physical examination he should be evaluated for the common hip dysplasia plus other diseases of the joints. There are tests to assist in the prediction of these problems. Other tests can also be run, such as the par-

Genetic predisposition to hip dysplasia and skin problems can easily be passed from mother to puppy.

vovirus antibody titer, which can assess the effectiveness of the vaccination programme.

Unless you intend to breed or show your dog, neutering the puppy at six months of age is recommended. Discuss this with your veterinary surgeon.

By the time your German Shepherd Dog is seven or eight months of age, he can be seriously evaluated for his conformation to the club standard, thus determining its show potential and its desirability as a sire or dam. If the puppy is not top class and therefore is not a candidate for a serious breeding programme, most professionals advise neutering the puppy. Neutering has proven to be extremely beneficial to both male and female puppies. Besides the obvious impossibility of pregnancy, it inhibits (but does not prevent) breast cancer in bitches and prostate cancer in male dogs.

Blood tests are performed for heartworm infestation and it is possible

DID YOU KNOW?

As German Shepherd puppies become more and more expensive, especially those puppies of high quality for showing and/or breeding, they have a greater chance of being stolen. The usual collar dog tag is, of course, easily removed. But there are two techniques which are becoming widely utilised for identification.

The puppy microchip implantation involves the injection of a small microchip, about the size of a corn kernel, under the skin of the dog. If your dog shows up at a clinic or shelter, or is offered for resale under less than savory circumstances, it can be positively identified by the microchip. The microchip is scanned and a registry quickly identifies you as the owner. This is not only protection against theft, but should the dog run away or go chasing a varmint and get lost, you have a fair chance of getting it back.

Tattooing is done on various parts of the dog, from its belly to its cheeks. The number tattooed can be your telephone number or any other number which you can easily memorise. When professional dog thieves see a tattooed dog, they usually lose interest in it. Both microchipping and tattooing can be done at your local veterinary clinic. For the safety of our German Shepherd Dogs, no laboratory facility or dog broker will accept a tattooed dog as stock.

that your puppy will be placed on a preventative therapy which will prevent heartworm infection as well as control other internal parasites.

DOGS OLDER THAN ONE YEAR

Continue to visit the veterinary surgeon at least once a year. There is no such disease as *old age*, but bodily functions do change with age, and the eyes and ears are no longer as efficient. Neither are the internal workings of the liver, kidneys and intestines. Proper dietary changes, recommended by your veterinary surgeon, can make life more pleasant for the aging German Shepherd Dog and you.

SKIN PROBLEMS IN GERMAN SHEPHERD DOGS

Veterinary surgeons are consulted by dog owners for skin problems more than any other group of diseases or maladies. Dogs' skin is almost as sensitive as human skin and both suffer almost the same maladies. (Though the occurrence of acne in dogs is rare!) For this reason, veterinary dermatology has developed into a specialty practiced by many veterinary surgeons.

Since many skin problems have visual symptoms which are almost identical, it requires the skill of an experienced veterinary dermatologist to identify and cure many of the more severe skin disorders. Simply put, if your dog is suffering from a

Dogs who spend times in woodsy areas are prone to parasites and other possible skin problems.

97

skin disorder, seek professional assistance as quickly as possible. As with all diseases, the earlier a problem is identified and treated, the more successful is the cure.

Pet shops sell many treatments for skin problems. Most of the treatments are simply directed at symptoms and not the underlying problem(s).

INHERITED SKIN PROBLEMS

Many skin disorders are inherited and some are fatal. Acrodermatitis is an inherited disease which is transmitted by BOTH parents. The

DID YOU KNOW?

There is a 4:1 chance of a puppy getting this fatal gene combination from two parents with recessive genes for acrodermatitis:

AA= NORMAL, HEALTHY
aa= FATAL
Aa= RECESSIVE, NORMAL APPEARING

If the female parent has an Aa gene and the male parent has an Aa gene, the chances are one in four that the puppy will have the fatal genetic combination aa.

	Dam ♀	
	A	a
Sire ♂ A	AA	Aa
a	Aa	aa

DO YOU KNOW ABOUT HIP DYSPLASIA?

Hip dysplasia is a fairly common condition found in German Shepherd Dogs, as well as other large breeds. When a dog has hip dysplasia, its hind leg has an incorrectly formed hip joint. By constant use of the hip joint, it becomes more and more loose, wears abnormally and may become arthritic.

Hip dysplasia can only be confirmed with an X-ray, but certain symptoms may indicate a problem. Your German Shepherd Dog may have a hip dysplasia problem if it walks in a peculiar manner, hops instead of smoothly running, uses his hinds legs in unison (to keep the pressure off the weak joint), has trouble getting up from a prone position and always sits with both legs together on one side of its body.

As the dog matures, it may adapt well to life with a bad hip, but in a few years the arthritis develops and many German Shepherd Dogs with hip dysplasia become cripples.

Hip dysplasia is considered an inherited disease and can usually be diagnosed when the dog is three to nine months old. Some experts claim that a special diet might help your puppy outgrow the bad hip, but the usual treatments are surgical. The removal of the pectineus muscle, the removal of the round part of the femur, reconstructing the pelvis and replacing the hip with an artificial one. All of these surgical interventions are expensive, but they are usually very successful. Follow the advice of your veterinary surgeon.

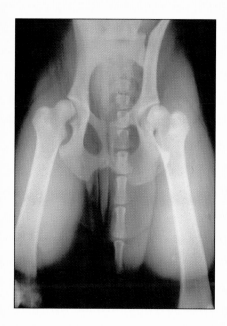

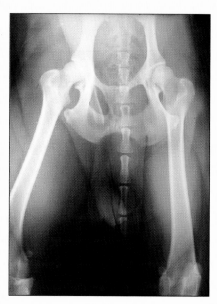

Compare the two hip joints and you'll understand dysplasia. Hip dysplasia is a badly worn hip joint caused by improper fit of the bone into the socket. It is easily the most common hip problem in German Shepherd Dogs.

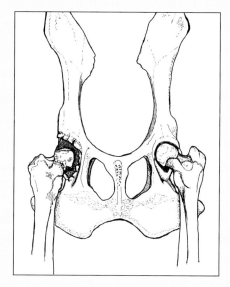

The healthy hip joint on the right and the unhealthy hip joint on the left.

Hip dysplasia can only be positively diagnosed by x-ray. German Shepherd Dogs manifest the problem when they are between four and nine months of age, the so-called fast growth period.

parents, which appear (phenotypically) normal, have a recessive gene for acrodermatitis, meaning that they carry, but are not affected by the disease.

Dogs can be allergic to their food.

Acrodermatitis is just one example of how difficult it is to diagnose and treat many dog diseases. The cost and skills required to ascertain whether two dogs should be mated is too high even though puppies with acrodermatitis rarely reach two years of age.

Other inherited skin problems are usually not as fatal as acrodermatitis. All inherited diseases must be diagnosed and treated by a veterinary

specialist. There are active programmes being undertaken by many veterinary pharmaceutical manufacturers to solve most, if not all, of the common skin problems of dogs.

PARASITE BITES

Many of us are allergic to mosquito bites. The bites itch, erupt and may even become infected. Dogs have the same reaction to fleas, ticks and/or mites. When you feel the prick of the mosquito when it bites you, you have a chance to kill it with your hand. Unfortunately, when our dog is bitten by a flea, tick or mite, it can only scratch it away or bite it. By the time the dog has been bitten, the parasite has done some of its damage. It may also have laid eggs to cause further problems in the near future. The itching from parasite bites is probably due to the saliva injected into the site when the parasite sucks the dog's blood.

AIRBORNE ALLERGIES

Another interesting allergy is pollen allergy. Humans have hay fever, rose fever and other fevers with which they suffer during the pollinating season. Many dogs suffer the same allergies. So when the pollen count

Your German Shepherd's skin and coat should be checked often for any sign of irritation, especially after he has been outdoors.

> **DID YOU KNOW?**
> Chances are that you and your dog will have the same allergies. Your allergies are readily recognizable and usually easily treated. Your dog's allergies may be masked.

are very susceptible to airborne pollen allergies.

Dogs, like humans, can be tested for allergens. Discuss the testing with your veterinary dermatologist.

FOOD ALLERGIES

Dogs are allergic to many foods which are best-sellers and highly recommended by breeders and veterinary surgeons. Changing the brand of food that you buy may not eliminate the problem because the element of the food to which the dog is allergic may also be contained in the new brand.

Recognizing a food allergy is difficult. Humans vomit or have rashes when they eat a food to which they are allergic. Dogs neither vomit nor

is high, your dog might suffer. Don't expect them to sneeze and have runny noses like humans. Dogs react to pollen allergies the same way they react to fleas—they scratch and bite themselves. German Shepherd Dogs

Disease	What is it?	What causes it?	Symptoms
Leptospirosis	Severe disease that affects the internal organs; can be spread to people.	A bacterium, which is often carried by rodents, that enters through mucous membranes and spreads quickly throughout the body.	Range from fever, vomiting and loss of appetite in less severe cases to shock, irreversible kidney damage and possibly death in most severe cases.
Rabies	Potentially deadly virus that infects warm-blooded mammals. Not seen in United Kingdom.	Bite from a carrier of the virus, mainly wild animals.	1st stage: dog exhibits change in behaviour, fear. 2nd stage: dog's behaviour becomes more aggressive. 3rd stage: loss of coordination, trouble with bodily functions.
Parvovirus	Highly contagious virus, potentially deadly.	Ingestion of the virus, which is usually spread through the faeces of infected dogs.	Most common: severe diarrhoea. Also vomiting, fatigue, lack of appetite.
Kennel cough	Contagious respiratory infection.	Combination of types of bacteria and virus. Most common: *Bordetella bronchiseptica* bacteria and parainfluenza virus.	Chronic cough.
Distemper	Disease primarily affecting respiratory and nervous system.	Virus that is related to the human measles virus.	Mild symptoms such as fever, lack of appetite and mucous secretion progress to evidence of brain damage, 'hard pad.'
Hepatitis	Virus primarily affecting the liver.	Canine adenovirus type I (CAV-1). Enters system when dog breathes in particles.	Lesser symptoms include listlessness, diarrhoea, vomiting. More severe symptoms include 'blue-eye' (clumps of virus in eye).
Coronavirus	Virus resulting in digestive problems.	Virus is spread through infected dog's faeces.	Stomach upset evidenced by lack of appetite, vomiting, diarrhoea.

(usually) develop a rash. Instead they itch, scratch and bite, thus making the diagnosis extremely difficult. While pollen allergies and parasite bites are usually seasonal, food allergies are year-round problems.

TREATING FOOD PROBLEMS

Handling food allergies and food intolerance yourself is possible. Put your dog on a diet which it has never had. Obviously if it never ate this new food it can't have been allergic or intolerant of it. Start with a single ingredient which is NOT in the dog's diet at the present time. Ingredients like chopped beef or fish are common in dog's diets, so try something more exotic like ostrich, rabbit, pheasant or even just vegetables such as potatoes. Keep the dog on this diet (with no additives) for a month. If the symptoms of food allergy or intolerance disappear, chances are that you have defined the cause.

A scanning electron micrograph of a dog flea, Ctenocephalides canis, *enlarged about 30X.*

Don't think that the single ingredient cured the problem. You still must find a suitable diet and ascertain which ingredient in the old diet was objectionable. This is most easily done by adding ingredients to the new diet one at a time until the problem is solved. Let the dog stay on the modified diet for a month before you add another ingredient.

An alternative method is to carefully study the ingredients in the diet to which your dog is allergic or intolerable. Identify the main ingredient in this diet and eliminate the main ingredient by buying a different food which does not have that ingredient. Keep experimenting until the symptoms disappear after one month on the new diet.

EXTERNAL PARASITES

Of all the problems to which dogs are prone, none is more well known and frustrating than fleas. *Fleas,* which usually refers to fleas, ticks and mites, are relatively simple to cure but difficult to prevent. The opposite is true for the parasites which are harboured inside the body. They are a bit more difficult to cure but they are easier to control.

S. E. M. BY DR. DENNIS KUNKEL, UNIVERSITY OF HAWAII.

FLEAS

It is possible to control flea infestation but you have to understand the life cycle of a typical flea in order to control them. Basically fleas are a summertime problem and their effective treatment (destruction) is environmental. The problem is that there is no single flea control medicine (insecticide) which can be used in every flea infested area. To understand flea control you must apply suitable treatment to the weak link in the life cycle of the flea.

A scanning electron micrograph of a dog or cat flea, Ctenocephalides enlarged about 100X. This has been coloured for effect.

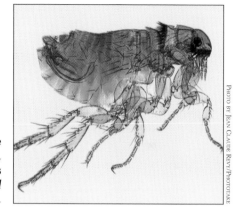

Photo by Jean Claude Revy/Phototake

A male dog flea, Ctenocephalides canis, *enlarged about 50X.*

The Life Cycle of a Flea

Fleas are found in four forms: eggs, larvae, pupae and adults. You really need a low-power microscope or hand lens to identify a living flea's eggs, pupae or larva. They spend their whole lives on your German Shepherd Dog unless they are forcibly removed by brushing, bathing, scratching or biting.

Several species infest both dog and cats. The dog flea is scientifically known as *Ctenocephalides*

The eggs of the dog flea.

Male cat fleas, Ctenocephalides felis, *are very commonly found on dogs.*

DID YOU KNOW?

Average size dogs, like German Shepherd Dogs, can pass 1,360,000 roundworm eggs every day.

With an average of 1 million German Shepherd Dogs in the world, the world is saturated with 1,300 metric tonnes of dog faeces.

These faeces contain 15,000,000,000 roundworm eggs.

7-31% of home gardens and children's play boxes in the U. S. contained roundworm eggs.

Flushing dog's faeces down the toilet is not a safe practice because the usual sewage treatments do not destroy roundworm eggs.

Infected German Shepherd puppies start shedding roundworm eggs at 3 weeks of age. They can be infected by their mother's milk.

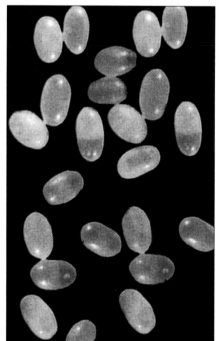

Photo by Jean Claude Revy/Phototake

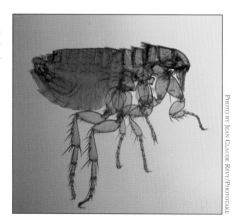

The Life Cycle of the Flea

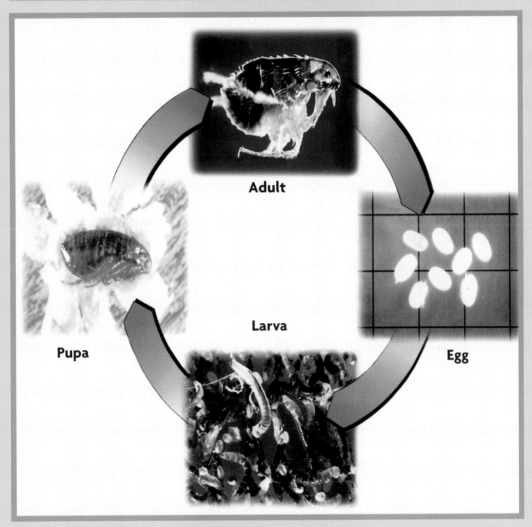

Adult

Pupa

Larva

Egg

The Life Cycle of the Flea was posterized by Fleabusters. Poster courtesy of Fleabusters®, Rx for Fleas.

Dwight R. Kuhn's magnificent action photo showing a flea jumping from a dog's back.

PHOTO BY DWIGHT R. KUHN

DID YOU KNOW?

Fleas have been around for millions of years and have adapted to changing host animals.

They are able to go through a complete life cycle in less than one month or they can extend their lives to almost two years by remaining as pupae or cocoons. They do not need blood or any other food for up to 20 months.

They have been measured as being able to jump 300,000 times and can jump 150 times their length in any direction including straight up. Those are just a few of the reasons they are so successful in infesting a dog!

canis while the cat flea is *Cteno-cephalides felis.* Cat fleas are very common on dogs.

Fleas lay eggs while they are in residence on your dog. These eggs

Dogs pick up fleas outdoors, too.

The head of a dog flea, Ctenocephalides *canis, enlarged about 165X.*

do not adhere to the hair of your dog and they simply fall off almost as soon as they dry (they may be a bit damp when initially laid). These eggs are the reservoir of future flea infestations. If your dog scratches himself and is able to dislodge a few fleas, they simply fall off and

await a future chance to attack a dog...or even a person. *Yes, fleas from dogs bite people.* That's why it is so important to control fleas both on the dog and in the dog's entire environment. You must, therefore, treat the dog and the environment simultaneously.

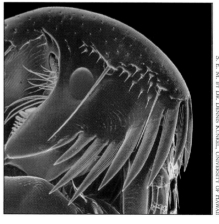

S. E. M. BY DR. DENNIS KINZEL, UNIVERSITY OF HAWAII

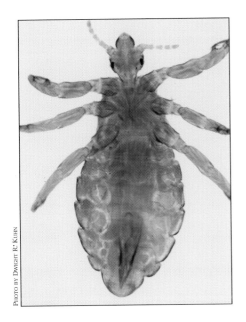

Photo by Dwight R. Kuhn

Human lice look like dog lice; the two are closely related.

DE-FLEAING THE HOME

Cleanliness is the simple rule. If you have a cat living with your dog, the matter is more complicated since most dog fleas are actually cat fleas. But since cats climb onto many areas that are never accessible to dogs (like window sills, table tops, etc.), you have to clean all of these areas, too. The hard floor surfaces (tiles, wood, stone and linoleum) must be mopped several times a day. Drops of food onto the floor are actually food for flea larvae! All rugs and furniture must be vacuumed several times a day. Don't forget closets, under furniture, cushions. A study has reported that a vacuum cleaner with a beater bar can only remove 20% of the larvae and 50% of the eggs. The vacuum bags should be discarded into a sealed plastic bag or burned. The vacuum machine itself should be cleaned. The outdoor area to which your dog has access must also be treated with an insecticide.

This all sounds like a lot of work! It is and, therefore, if you can afford it, you are better off hiring a professional to do it.

While there are many drugs available to kill fleas on the dog itself, such as the miracle drug ivermectin, it is best to have the de-fleaing and de-worming supervised by your vet. Ivermectin is effective against many external and internal parasites including heartworms, roundworms, tapeworms, flukes, ticks and mites. It has not been approved for use to control these pests, but veterinary surgeons frequently use it anyway.

De-fleaing your dog is easy, it's ridding the surrounding environment of fleas that is difficult.

STERILISING THE ENVIRONMENT

Besides cleaning your home with vacuum cleaners and mops, you have to treat the outdoor range of your dog. This means trimming bushes, spreading insecticide and being careful not to poison areas in which fishes or other animals reside.

107

The dog tick, Dermacentor variabilis, *is probably the most common tick found on dogs. Look at the strength in its eight legs! No wonder it's hard to detach them.*

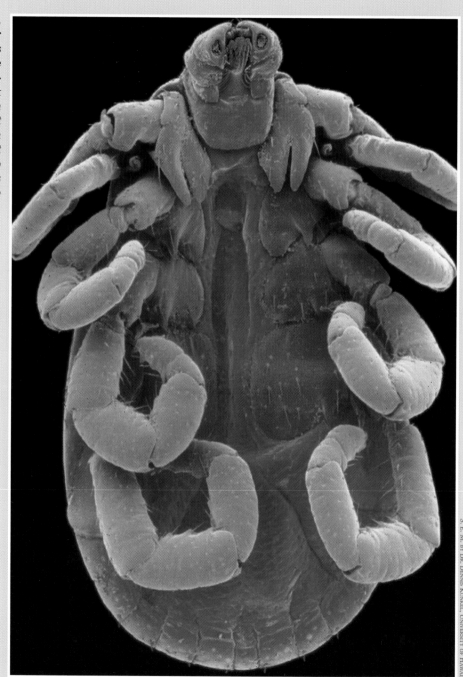

This is best done by an outside service specialising in de-fleaing. Your vet should be able to recommend a local service.

TICKS AND MITES

Though not as common as fleas, ticks and mites are found all over the tropical and temperate world. They don't bite, like fleas, rather they harpoon. They dig their sharp

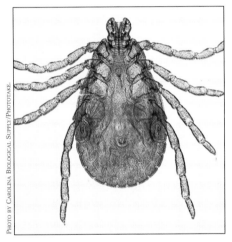

The head of the dog tick, Dermacentor variabilis, *enlarged 90X.*

A brown dog tick, Rhipicephalus sanguineus, *is an uncommon but annoying tick frequently found on German Shepherd Dogs.*

The dog tick *Dermacentor variabilis* may well be the most common dog tick in many geographical areas, especially those areas where the climate is hot and humid.

Most dog ticks have life expectancies of a week to six months, depending upon climatic conditions. They can neither jump

proboscis (nose) into the dog's skin and drink the blood. Their only food and drink is dog's blood. Dogs can get Lyme disease, Rocky Mountain spotted fever (normally found in the U.S.A. only), paralysis and many other maladies, from ticks and mites. They may live where fleas are found except they like to hide in cracks or seams in walls wherever dogs live. They are controlled the same way fleas are controlled.

The dog tick of the genus Ixode *enlarged 10X.*

109

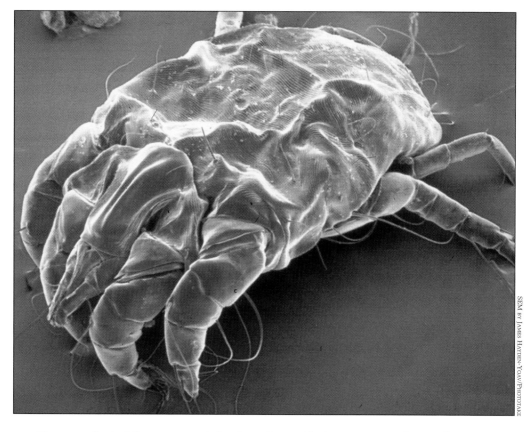

The mange mite, Psoroptes bovis, enlarged more than 200X.

nor fly, but they can crawl slowly and can range up to 5 metres (16 feet) to reach a sleeping or unsuspecting dog.

MANGE

Mites cause a skin irritation called *mange.* Some are contagious, like *Cheyletiella, ear mites, scabies and chiggers.* The non-contagious mites are Demodex. The most serious of the mites is the ear mite infestation. Ear mites are usually controlled with ivermectin.

It is essential that your dog be treated for mange as quickly as possi-

ble because some forms of mange are transmissible to people.

AUTO-IMMUNE SKIN CONDITIONS

Auto-immune skin conditions are commonly referred to as being allergic to yourself. Allergies, though, usually result in inflammatory reactions to an outside stimulus. Auto-immune diseases cause serious damage to the tissues which are involved.

The best known auto-immune disease is lupus. It affects people as well as dogs. The symptoms are very variable and may affect the kidneys, bones, blood chemistry and skin. It can be fatal to both dogs and humans, though it is not thought to be transmissible. It is usually successfully treated with cortisone, prednisone or similar corticosteroid, but extensive use of these drugs can have harmful side effects.

ACRAL LICK DISEASE

German Shepherd Dogs and other dogs about the same size (like Labrador Retrievers), have a very poorly understood syndrome called *acral lick*. The manifestation of the problem is the dog's tireless attack at a specific area of the body, almost always the legs. They lick so intensively that they remove the hair and skin leaving an ugly, large wound. There is no absolute cure, but corticosteroids are the most common treatment.

Acral lick syndrome results in a large open wound, a lick granuloma, usually on the dog's leg.

INTERNAL PARASITES

Most animals—fishes, birds and mammals, including dogs and humans—have worms and other parasites which

SEM BY JAMES HAYDEN-YOAV/PHOTOTAKE

The dog mange mite is frequently seen on cows as well. Enlarged about 300X.

DID YOU KNOW?

There are many parasiticides which can be used around your home and garden to control fleas.

Natural pyrethrins can be used inside the house.

Allethrin, bioallethrin, permethrin and resmethrin can also be used inside the house but permethrin has been used successfully outdoors, too.

Carbaryl can be used indoors and outdoors.

Propxur can be used indoors.

Chlorpyrifos, diazinon and malathion can be used indoors or outdoors and it has an extended residual activity.

live inside their bodies. According to Dr. Herbert R. Axelrod, the fish pathologist, there are two kinds of parasites: dumb and smart. The smart parasites live in peaceful cooperation with their hosts (symbiosis), while the dumb parasites kill their host. Most of the worm infections are relatively easy to control. If they are not controlled they eventually weaken the host dog to the point that other medical problems occur, but they are not dumb parasites.

ROUNDWORMS

The roundworms that infect dogs are scientifically known as *Toxocara canis*. They live in the dog's intestine. The worms shed eggs continually. It

The round-worm can infect both dogs and humans. Enlarged about 175X.

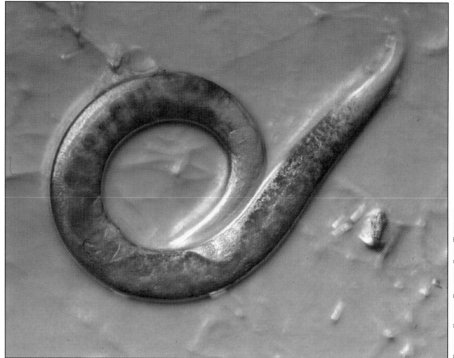

has been estimated that a German Shepherd Dog produces about 150 grammes of faeces every day. Each gramme of faeces averages 10,000-12,000 eggs of roundworms. There are no known areas in which dogs roam that does not contain the eggs of roundworms. The greatest danger of roundworms is that they infect people, too! It is wise to have your dog tested regularly for roundworms.

Pigs also have roundworm infections which can be passed to human and dogs. The typical roundworm parasite is called *Ascaris lumbricoides.*

HOOKWORMS

The worm *Ancylostoma caninum* is commonly called the dog hookworm. It is dangerous to humans and cats. It also has teeth by which it attaches itself to the intestines of the dog. Because it changes the site of its attachment about six times a day, the dog loses blood from each detach-

DID YOU KNOW?

Humans, rats, squirrels, foxes, coyotes, wolves, mixed breeds of dogs and purebred dogs are all susceptible to tapeworm infection. Except for humans, tapeworms are usually not a fatal infection.

Infected individuals can harbour a thousand parasitic worms.

Tapeworms have two sexes—male and female (many other worms have only one sex—male and female in the same worm).

If dogs eat infected rats or mice, they get the tapeworm disease.

One month after attaching to a dog's intestine, the worm starts shedding eggs. These eggs are infective immediately.

Infective eggs can live for a few months without a host animal.

Roundworms, hookworms, whipworms and tapeworms are just a few of the commonly known worms which infect dogs.

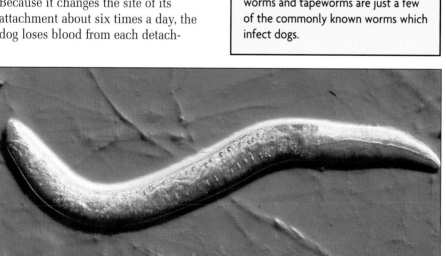

The round-worm, Ascaris lumbricoides, *is found in dogs, pigs and humans.*

The roundworm Rhabditis.

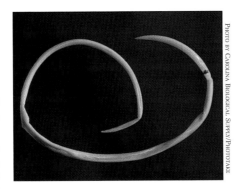

Photo by Carolina Biological Supply/Phototake

Male and female hookworms, Ancylostoma caninum, found in German Shepherd Dogs.

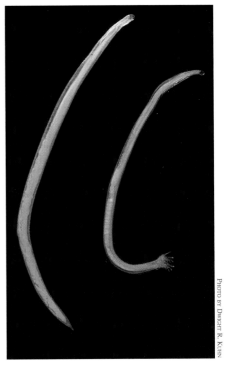

Photo by Dwight R. Kuhn

DID YOU KNOW?

Ivermectin is quickly becoming the drug of choice for treating many parasitic skin diseases in dogs.

For some unknown reason, herding dogs like German Shepherd Dogs, Collies, Old English Sheepdogs, Australian Shepherds, etc., are extremely sensitive to ivermectin.

Ivermectin injections have killed some dogs, but dogs heavily infected with skin disorders may be treated anyway.

The ivermectin reaction is a toxicosis which causes tremors, loss of power to move their muscles, prolonged dilitation of the pupil of the eye, coma (unconsciousness), or cessation of breathing (death).

The toxicosis usually starts from 4-6 hours after ingestion (not injection), or as late as 12 hours. The longer it takes to set in, the milder is the reaction.

Ivermectin should only be prescribed and administered by a vet.

Some ivermectin treatments require two doses.

ment, possibly causing iron-deficiency anaemia. They are easily purged from the dog with many medications, the best of which seems to be ivermectin even though it has not been approved for such use.

TAPEWORMS

There are many species of tapeworms. They are carried by fleas! The dog eats the flea and thus starts the tapeworm cycle. Humans can also be infected with tapeworms, so don't eat fleas! Fleas are so small that your dog could pass them onto your hands, your plate or your food and thus make it possible for you to ingest a flea which is carrying tapeworm eggs.

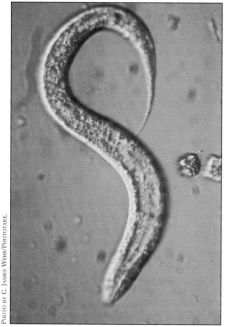

The infective stage of the hookworm larva. Enlarged 1,000X.

While tapeworm infection is not life threatening in dogs (smart parasite!), it can be the cause of a very serious liver disease for humans. About 50 percent of the humans infected with *Echinococcus multilocularis*, causing alveolar hydatis, perish.

HEARTWORMS

Heartworms are thin, extended worms up to 30 cm (12 in.) long which live in

The head and rostellum (the round prominence on the scolex) of a tapeworm, which infects dogs and humans.

DID YOU KNOW?

There are drugs which prevent fleas from maturing from egg to adult.

The weak link is the maturation from a larva to a pupa.

Methoprene and fenoxycarb mimic the effect of maturation enhancers, thus, in effect, killing the larva before it pupates.

Methoprene is very effective in killing flea eggs while fenoxycarb is better able to stand UV rays from the sun. There is a combination of both drugs which has an effective life of 6 months and destroys 93% of the flea population.

It is important, in order to effectively control fleas, that you use products designed to kill fleas at all stages of growth, Manufacturers make such products, which are specifically designed for this purpose, and specially made to be safe for use in the home and on the dog.

PHOTO BY C. JAMES WEBB/PHOTOTAKE.

PHOTO BY CAROLINA BIOLOGICAL SUPPLY/PHOTOTAKE.

The heartworm, Dirofilaria immitis.

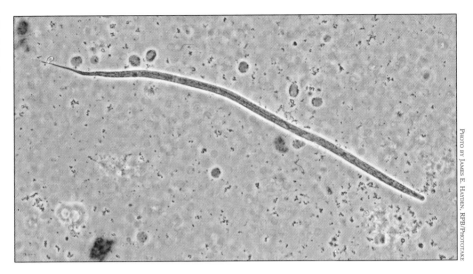

PHOTO BY JAMES E. HAYDEN, RPB/PHOTOTAKE

DID YOU KNOW?

Dog food must be at room temperature, neither too hot nor too cold. Fresh water, changed daily and served in a clean bowl, is mandatory, especially when feeding dry food.

Never feed your dog from the table while you are eating. Never feed your dog left-overs from your own meal. They usually contain too much fat and too much seasoning.

Dogs must chew their food. Hard pellets are excellent; soups and slurries are to be avoided.

Don't add left-overs or any extras to normal dog food. The normal food is usually balanced and adding something extra destroys the balance.

Except for age-related changes, German Shepherd Dogs do not require dietary variations. They should be fed the same diet, day after day, without their becoming bored or ill.

a dog's heart and major blood vessels around the heart. German Shepherd Dogs may have to 200 of these worms. The symptoms may be loss of energy, loss of appetite, coughing, the development of a pot belly and anaemia.

Heartworms are transmitted by mosquitoes. The mosquito drinks the blood of an infected dog and takes in larvae with the blood. The larvae, called microfilaria, develop within the body of the mosquito and are passed on to the next dog bitten after the larvae mature. It takes two to three weeks for the larvae to develop to the infective stage within the body of the mosquito. Dogs should be treated at about six weeks of age, then every six months.

Blood testing for heartworms is not necessarily indicative of how seriously your dog is infected. This is a dangerous disease. Dogs in the United Kingdom are not affected by heartworm.

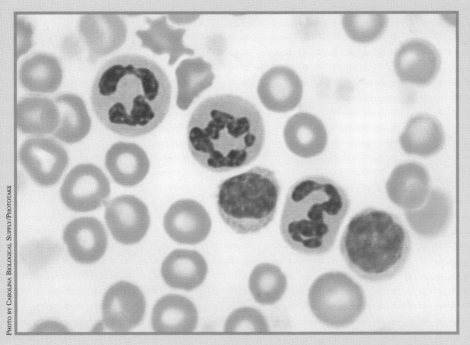

PHOTO BY CAROLINA BIOLOGICAL SUPPLY/PHOTOTAKE

Heartworm larvae, Dirofilaria immitis. Enlarged about 1,400X.

PHOTO BY JAMES E. HAYDEN, RPB/PHOTOTAKE

The heart of a dog infected with canine heartworm, Dirofilaria immitis.

A little grey around the muzzle doesn't keep the senior German Shepherd from being a loyal and loving pet.

When Your German Shepherd Dog Gets Old

The term *old* is a qualitative term. For dogs, as well as their masters, *old* is relative. Certainly we can all distinguish between a puppy German Shepherd and an adult German Shepherd—there are the obvious physical traits such as size and

appearance, and personality traits like their antics and the expressions on their faces. Puppies that are nasty are very rare. Puppies and young dogs like to play with children. Children's natural exuberance is a good match for the seemingly endless energy of young dogs. They like to run, jump, chase and retrieve. When dogs grow up and cease their interaction with children, they are often thought of as

being too old to play with the kids.

On the other hand, if a German Shepherd is only exposed to people over 60 years of age, its life will

Old dogs lose their natural exuberance.

normally be less active and it will not seem to be *getting old* as soon as its activity level slows down.

If people live to be 100 years old, dogs live to be 20 years old. While this is a good rule of thumb, it is VERY inaccurate. When trying

Hair around the face and paws starts to turn grey as the German Shepherd Dog enters his senior years.

DID YOU KNOW?
The bottom line is simply that a dog is getting old when YOU think it is getting old because it slows down in its general activities, including walking, running, eating, jumping and retrieving. On the other hand, certain activities increase, like more sleeping, more licking your hands and body, more barking and more repetition of habits like going to the door when you put your coat on without being called.

to compare dog years to human years, you cannot make a generalisation about all dogs. You can make the generalisation that, say, 13 years is a good life span for a German Shepherd, but you cannot compare it to that of a Chihuahua, as many small breeds typically live longer than large breeds. Dogs are generally considered mature within three years. They can reproduce even earlier. So the first three years of a dog's life are more like seven times that of comparable humans. That means a three-year-old dog is like a 21-year-old person. As the curve of comparison shows, there is no hard and fast rule for comparing dog and human ages. The comparison is made even more difficult, for not all humans age

DID YOU KNOW?
An old dog starts to show one or more of the following symptoms:

• The hair on its face and paws starts to turn grey. The colour breakdown usually starts around the eyes and mouth.

• The exercise routine becomes more and more tedious and the dog almost refuses to join exercises that it previously enjoyed.

• Food intake diminishes.

• Responses to calls, whistles and other signals are ignored more and more.

• Eye contacts indicate aloofness and do not evoke tail wagging (assuming they always did).

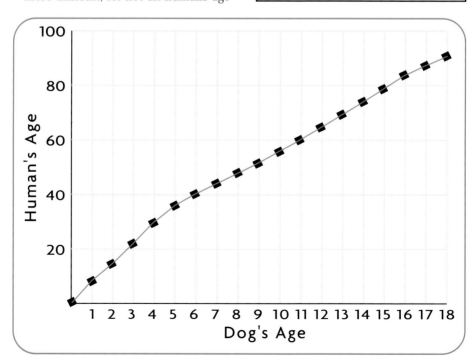

DID YOU KNOW?
The symptoms listed below are symptoms that gradually appear and gradually become more noticeable. They are not life threatening, however, the symptoms below are to be taken very seriously and a discussion with your veterinary surgeon is warranted:

• Your dog cries and whimpers when it moves and stops running completely.

• Convulsions start or become more serious and frequent. The usual convulsion (spasm) is when the dog stiffens and starts to tremble being unable or unwilling to move. The seizure usually lasts for 5 to 30 minutes.

• More and more toilet accidents occur. Urine and bowel movements take place indoors without warning.

• Vomiting becomes more and more frequent.

at the same rate...and human females live longer than human males.

WHAT TO DO WHEN THE TIME COMES

You are never fully prepared to make a rational decision about putting your dog to sleep. It is very obvious that you love your German Shepherd or you would not be reading this book. Putting a loved dog to sleep is extremely difficult. It is a decision that must be made with your veterinary surgeon. You are usually forced to make the decision when one of the life-threatening symptoms listed above becomes serious enough for

you to seek medical (veterinary) help.

If the prognosis of the malady indicates the end is near and your beloved pet will only suffer more and experience no enjoyment for the balance of its life, then there is no choice but euthanasia.

WHAT IS EUTHANASIA?

Euthanasia derives from the Greek meaning *good death*. In other words, it means the planned, painless killing of a dog suffering from a painful, incurable condition, or who is so aged that it cannot walk, see, eat or control its excretory functions.

Euthanasia is usually accomplished by injection with an overdose of an anaesthesia or barbiturate. Aside from the prick of the needle, the experience is painless.

HOW ABOUT YOU?

The days during which the dog becomes ill and the end occurs can be unusually stressful for you. If this is your first experience with the death of a loved one, you may need the comfort dictated by your religious beliefs. If you are the head of the family and have children, you should have

DID YOU KNOW?
Euthanasia must be done by a licensed veterinary surgeon. There also may be societies for the prevention of cruelty to animals in your area. They often offer this service upon a vet's recommendation. You should NEVER attempt euthanasia by yourself.

involved them in the decision of putting your German Shepherd to sleep. In any case, euthanasia alone is painful and stressful for the family of

Loss of your beloved dog is a sorrowful experience for the whole family.

the dog. Unfortunately, it does not end there. The decision-making process is just as hard.

Usually your dog can be maintained on drugs for a few days while it is kept in the clinic in order to give you ample time to make a decision. During this time, talking with members of the family or religious repre-

sentatives, or even people who have lived through this same experience, can ease the burden of your inevitable decision...but then what?

HOW ABOUT THE FINAL RESTING PLACE?
Dogs can have the same privileges as humans. They can be buried in their entirety in a pet cemetery (very expensive) in a burial container, buried in your garden in a place suitably marked with a stone or newly planted tree or bush, cremated with the ashes being given to you, or even stuffed and mounted by a taxidermist.

All of these options should be discussed frankly and openly with your veterinary surgeon. Do not be afraid to ask financial questions. Cremations are usually mass burning and the ashes you get may not be the ashes of your beloved dog. There are

If you are interested in locating a pet cemetery for your deceased dog, your vet may be of assistance.

very small crematories available to all veterinary clinics. If you want a private cremation, your vet can usually arrange it. However, this may be a little more expensive.

GETTING ANOTHER DOG?

The grief of losing your beloved dog will be as lasting as the grief of losing a human friend or relative. You

> **DID YOU KNOW?**
> The more open discussion you have about the whole stressful occurrence, the easier it will be for you when the time comes.

cannot go out and buy another grandfather, but you can go out and buy another German Shepherd. In most cases, if your dog died of *old age* (if there is such a thing), it had slowed down considerably. Do you want a new German Shepherd puppy to replace it? Or are you better off in finding a more mature German Shepherd, say two to three years of age, which will usually be housebroken and will have an already developed personality. In this case, you can find out if you like each other after a few hours of being together.

The decision is, of course, your own. Do you want another German Shepherd? Perhaps you want a smaller or larger dog? How much do you want to spend on a dog? Look in your local newspapers for advertisements (*DOGS FOR SALE*), or, better

yet, consult your local society for the prevention of cruelty to animals to adopt a dog. Pet shops may be the most convenient place from which to buy a puppy. They are usually regulated by local laws, they worry about their reputation, they almost always will take a dog back with seven days if your veterinary surgeon discovers a malady or deformity, and they usually are the least expensive option because they have the lowest quality dogs when judged according to the breed's standards. Private dog kennels specialising in a particular breed are the source for high-quality dogs that they usually breed from champion stock.

Whatever you decide, do it as quickly as possible. Most people usually buy the same breed they had before because they know (and love) the characteristics of that breed. Then, too, they often know people who have the same breed and perhaps they are lucky enough that one of their friends expects a litter soon. What could be better?

A resting place for your dog's ashes may be available locally. Your veterinary surgeon can probably help you.

Showing Your German Shepherd Dog

Is the puppy you selected growing into a handsome representative of his breed? You are rightly proud of your handsome little tyke, and he has mastered nearly all of the basic obedience commands that you have taught him. How about attending a dog show and seeing how the other half of the dog-loving world lives! Even if you never imagined yourself standing in the centre ring at the Crufts Dog Show, why not dream a little?

The first concept that the canine neophyte learns when watching a dog show is that each breed first competes against members of its own breed. Once the judge has selected the best member of each breed, then that chosen dog will compete with other dogs of his classification. Finally the best of each group will compete for Best of Show and Reserve winners.

The second concept that you must understand is that the dogs are not actually competing with one another. The judge compares each dog against the breed standard, which is a written description of the ideal specimen of the breed. This imaginary dog never walked into a

Did you buy your dog for show or fun?

show ring, has never been bred and, to the woe of dog breeders around the globe, does *not* exist. Breeders attempt to get as close to this ideal as possible, with every litter, but theoretically the 'perfect' dog is so elusive that it is impossible. (And if the 'perfect' dog were born, breeders and judges would never agree that it was indeed 'perfect.')

If you are interested in exploring dog shows, your best bet is to join your local breed club. These clubs host shows (often matches and open shows for beginners), send out newsletters, offer training days and provide an outlet to meet members

Dog shows in the U. S. are often held outdoors. These dogs are being run in front of the judges so their gaits can be evaluated.

who are often friendly and generous with their advice and contacts. To locate the nearest breed club for you, contact The Kennel Club, the ruling body for the British dog world, not just for conformation shows, but for working trials, obedience trials, agility trials and field trials. The Kennel Club furnishes the rules and regulations for all these events plus general dog registration and other basic requirements of dog ownership. Its annual show, held in Birmingham, is the largest bench show in England. Every year no fewer than 20,000 of the U.K.'s best dogs qualify to participate in a marvelous show lasting four days.

In shows held under the auspices of The Kennel Club, which includes Great Britain, Australia, South Africa and beyond, there are different kinds of shows. At the most competitive and prestigious of these shows, the Championship Shows, a dog can earn Challenge Certificates, and thereby become a 'champion.' A dog must earn three Challenge Certificates under three different judges to earn

the prefix of 'Sh Ch' or 'Ch.' Note that some breeds must qualify in a field trial in order to gain the title of full champion. Challenge Certificates are awarded to a very small percentage of the dogs competing, and the number of Challenge Certificates awarded in any one year is based upon the total number of dogs in each breed entered for competition. There two types of Championship Shows, a general show, where all breeds recognised by The Kennel Club can enter, and a breed show, which is limited to only a single breed.

Open Shows are generally less competitive and are frequently used as 'practice shows' for young dogs. These

---

WINNING THE TICKET

Earning a championship at Kennel Club shows is the most difficult in the world. Compared to the United States and Canada where it is relatively not 'challenging,' collecting three green tickets not only requires much time and effort, it can be very expensive! Challenge Certificates, as the tickets are properly known, are the building blocks of champions— good breeding, good handling, good training and good luck!

---

shows, of which there are hundreds each year, can be invitingly social events and are great first show experiences for the novice. If you're just considering watching a show to wet your paws, an Open Show is a great choice.

While Championship and Open Shows are most important for the beginner to understand, there are other types of shows in which the interested dog owner can participate. Training clubs, for example, sponsor Matches that can be entered on the day of the show for a nominal fee. These introductory level exhibitions are uniquely run: two dogs are pulled from a raffle and 'matched,' the winner of that match goes on to the next round, and eventually only one dog is left undefeated.

Exemption shows are similar in that they are simply fun classes and usually held in conjunction with small agricultural shows. Primary shows can also be entered on the day of the event and dogs entered must not have won anything towards their titles. Limited shows must be entered well in advance, and there are limitations upon who can enter. Beginners that are interested in showing their German Shepherds for the sake of experiencing the excitement of competing with others—and even taking home a ribbon or prize—should attend a Primary show. It is far better to begin at the simplest shows for the owner and dog alike. Regardless of which type

The German Shepherd Dog's conformation is based on function as well as form. The Kennel Club standard clearly states '...working ability is never sacrificed for mere beauty.'

127

show you choose to begin with, you and your dog will have a grand time competing and learning your way about the shows.

Before you actually step into the ring, you would be well advised to sit back and observe the judge's ring procedure. If it is your first time in the ring, do not be over-anxious and run to the front of the line. It is much better when you can stand back and study how the exhibitor in front of you is performing. The judge asks each handler to 'stand' the dog, hopefully showing the dog off to his best advantage. The judge will observe the dog from a distance and from different angles, approach the dog, check his teeth, overall structure, alertness and musculature, as

DID YOU KNOW?

Just like with anything else, there is a certain etiquette to the show ring that can only be learned through experience. Showing your dog can be quite intimidating to you as a novice when it seems as if everyone else knows what he's doing. You can familiarise yourself with ring procedure beforehand by taking a class to prepare you and your dog for conformation showing or by talking with an experienced handler. When you are in the ring, listen and pay attention to the judge and follow his/her directions. Remember, even the most skilled handlers had to start somewhere. Keep it up and you too will be a pro in no time!

If your dog isn't properly trained it will not be possible for you to show him. Your German Shepherd Dog must reliably obey your commands in the show ring in order to be successful.

well as consider how well the dog 'conforms' to the standard. Most importantly, the judge will have the exhibitor move the dog around the ring in some pattern that he or she should specify (another advantage to

not going first, but always listen since some judges change their directions, and the judge is always *right!*) Finally the judge will give the dog one last look before moving on to the next exhibitor.

If you are not in the top three at your first show, do not be discouraged. Be patient and consistent and you will eventually find yourself in the winning lineup. Remember that the winners were once in your shoes and have devoted many hours and much money to earn the placement. If you find that your dog is losing every time and never getting a nod, it may be time to consider a different dog sport or just to enjoy your German Shepherd as a pet.

WORKING TRIALS

Working trials can be entered by any well-trained dog of any breed, not just Gundogs or Working dogs. Many dogs that earn the Kennel Club Good Citizen Dog award choose to participate in a working trial. There are five stakes at both open and championship levels: Companion Dog (CD), Utility Dog (UD), Working Dog (WD), Tracking Dog (TD), and Patrol Dog (PD). Like in conformation shows, dogs compete against a standard and if the dog reaches the qualifying mark, it obtains a certificate. Divided into groups, each exercise must be achieved 70 percent in order to qualify. If the dog achieves 80 percent in the open level, it receives a Certificate of Merit (COM), in the championship level, it receives a Qualifying Certificate. At the CD stake, dogs must participate in four groups, Con-

Show dogs need to be properly groomed and in top condition for the ring.

trol, Stay, Agility and Search (Retrieve and Nosework). At the next three levels, UD, WD and TD, there are only three groups: Control, Agility and Nosework.

Agility consists of three jumps: a vertical scale, a six-foot wall of planks; a clear jump, a basic three-

Showing dogs can be big-time entertainment with expert handlers and beautiful dogs putting on quite a spectacle.

A champion German Shepherd Dog is not necessarily a better companion than a pet-quality dog. If you intend to show a dog, you will need professional assistance in acquiring a puppy with show potential.

foot hurdle with a removable top bar; and a long jump of angled planks stretching nine feet.

To earn the UD, WD and TD, dogs must track approximately one-half mile for articles laid from one-half hour to three hours ago. Tracks consist of turns and legs, and fresh ground is used for each participant.

The fifth stake, PD, involves teaching manwork, which of course is not recommended for every breed.

FIELD TRIALS AND WORKING TESTS

Working tests are frequently used to prepare dogs for field trials, the purpose of which is to heighten the instincts and natural abilities of gundogs. Live game is not used in working tests.

Unlike field trials, working tests do not count toward a dog's record at the Kennel Club, though the same judges often oversee working tests. Field trials began in England in 1947, and are only moderately popular among dog folk. While breeders of Working and Gundog breeds concern themselves with the field abilities of their dogs, there is considerably less interest in field trials than dog shows. In order for dogs to become full champions, certain breeds must qualify in the field as well. Upon gaining three CCs in the show ring, the dog is designated a Show Champion (Sh Ch). The title Champion (Ch) requires that the dog gain an award at a field trial, be a 'special qualifier' at a field trial or pass a 'special show dog qualifier' judged by a field trial judge on a shooting day.

Some owners participate in the Schutzhund trials with their German Shepherd Dogs. Schutzhund training is extremely rigorous and requires dedication to perfect the exercises.

AGILITY TRIALS

Agility trials began in the United Kingdom in 1977 and have since spread around the world, especially to the United States, where it enjoys strong popularity. The handler directs his dog over an obstacle course that includes jumps (such as those used in the working trials), as well as tyres, the dog walk, weave poles, pipe tunnels, collapsed tunnels, etc. The Kennel Club requires that dogs not be trained for agility until they are 12 months old. This dog sport intends to be great fun for dog and owner and interested owners should join a training club that has obstacles and experienced agility handlers who can introduce you and your dog to the 'ropes' (and tyres, tunnels and so on).

The judge compares the class of German Shepherds, which she has already examined individually.

CLASSES AT DOG SHOWS

There can be as many as 18 classes per sex for your breed. Check the show schedule carefully to make sure that you have entered your dog in the appropriate class. Among the classes offered can be: Minor Puppy (ages 6 to 9 months); Puppy (ages 6 to 12 months); Junior (ages 6 to 18 months); Beginners (handler or dog never won first place); as well as the following, each of which is defined in the schedule: Maiden; Novice; Tyro; Debutant; Undergraduate; Graduate; Postgraduate; Minor Limit; Mid Limit; Limit; Open; Veteran; Stud Dog; Brood Bitch; Progeny; Brace; and Team.

FÉDÉRATION CYNOLOGIQUE INTERNATIONALE

Established in 1911, the Fédération Cynologique Internationale represents the 'world kennel club,' the international body brings uniformity to the breeding, judging and showing of purebred dogs. Although the FCI originally included only European nations, namely France, Holland, Austria and Belgium, the latter of which remains the headquarters, the organisation today embraces nations on six continents and recognises well over 400 breeds of purebred dog. There are three titles attainable through the FCI: the International Champion, which is the most prestigious; the International Beauty Champion, which is based on aptitude certificates in different countries; and the International Trial Champion, which is based on achievement in obedience trials in different countries. Of course, quarantine laws in England and Australia prohibit most exhibitors from entering FCI shows,

133

A well-trained German Shepherd has learned how to stand politely in the ring whilst the judge examines him.

though the rest of the European Nation do participate in these impressive canine spectacles, the largest of which is the World Dog Show, hosted in a different country each year. FCI sponsors both national and international shows. The hosting country determines the judging system and breed standards are always based on the breed's country of origin.

HOW TO ENTER A DOG SHOW

1. Obtain an entry form and show schedule from the Show Secretary.
2. Select the classes that you want to enter and complete the entry form.
3. Transfer your dog into your name at The Kennel Club. (Be sure that this matter is handled before entering.)
4. Find out how far in advance show entries must be made. Oftentimes it's more than a couple of months.

DID YOU KNOW?

You can get information about dog shows from kennel clubs and breed clubs:

Fédération Cynologique Internationale
14, rue Leopold II, B-6530 Thuin, Belgium

The Kennel Club
1-5 Clarges St., Piccadilly, London W1Y 8AB, UK
www.the-kennel-club.org.uk

American Kennel Club
5580 Centerview Dr., Raleigh, NC 27606-3390, USA
www.akc.org

Canadian Kennel Club
89 Skyway Ave., Suite 100, Etobicoke, Ontario
M9W 6R4 Canada
www.ckc.ca

Verein für Deutsche Schäferhunde
Director C. Lux
Steinerne Furt 71/71 a, 86167 Augsburg, Germany
www.schaeferhunde.de

Dog shows take place world-wide, although many countries have quarantine laws inhibiting dog importation.

To best understand the way the German Shepherd behaves, an owner must learn to 'think like a dog.'

Understanding Your Dog's Behaviour

As a German Shepherd owner, you have selected your dog so that you and your loved ones can have a companion, a protector, a friend and a four-legged family member. You invest time, money and effort to care for and train the family's new charge. Of course, this chosen canine behaves perfectly! Well, perfectly like a *dog*.

THINK LIKE A DOG

Dogs do not think like humans, nor do humans think like dogs, though we try. Unfortunately, a dog is incapable of figuring out how humans think, so the responsibility falls on the owner to adopt a proper canine mindset. Dogs cannot rationalise, and dogs exist *in the present moment*. Many dog owners make the mistake in training of thinking that they can reprimand their dog for something he did a while ago. Basically, you cannot even reprimand a dog for something he did 20 seconds ago! Either catch him in the act or forget it! It is a waste of your and your dog's time—in his mind, you are reprimanding him for whatever he is doing at that moment.

The following behavioural problems represent some which owners

Get a group of German Shepherd Dogs together and one will always be alert and in charge. This same behaviour is true of many birds and animals. It is called the pecking order.

137

You have to be the dominant one, especially when more than one German Shepherd Dog is involved.

AGGRESSION

Aggression can be a very big problem in dogs. Aggression, when not controlled, becomes dangerous. An aggressive dog, no matter the size, may lunge at, bite or even attack a person or another dog. Aggressive behaviour is not to be tolerated. It is more than just inappropriate behaviour; it is not safe, especially with a large, powerful breed such as the German Shepherd. It is painful for a family to watch their dog become unpredictable in his behaviour to the point where they are afraid of the dog. And while not all aggressive behaviour is dangerous, it can be frightening: growling, baring teeth, etc. It is important to get to the root of the problem to ascertain why the dog is acting in this manner. Aggression is a display of dominance, and the dog should not have the dominant role in its pack, which is, in this case, your family.

It is important not to challenge an aggressive dog as this could provoke an attack. Observe your German Shepherd's body language. Does he make

most commonly encounter. Every dog is unique and every situation is unique. No author could purport to solve your German Shepherd's problem simply by reading a script. Here we outline some basic 'dogspeak' so that owners' chances of solving behavioural problems are increased. Discuss bad habits with your veterinary surgeon and he/she can recommend a behavioural specialist to consult in appropriate cases. Since behavioural abnormalities are the leading reason owners abandon their pets, we hope that you will make a valiant effort to solve your German Shepherd's problem. Patience and understanding are virtues that dwell in every pet-loving household.

A dog shows submission when it rolls over and exposes its stomach.

Bred for service to mankind, these two German Shepherds will pursue a career with the police. Fortunately they have an excellent start, having been bred by Meg Purnell-Carpenter of Overhill Kennels, home of National Police Champions as well as Kennel Club Champions.

direct eye contact and stare? Does he try to make himself as large as possible: ears pricked, chest out, tail erect? Height and size signify authority in a dog pack—being taller or 'above' another dog literally means that he is 'above' in the social status. These body signals tell you that your German Shepherd thinks he is in charge, a problem that needs to be dealt with. An aggressive dog is unpredictable in that you never know when he is going to strike and what he is going to do. You cannot understand why a dog that is playful and loving one minute is growling and snapping the next.

The best solution is to consult a behavioural specialist, one who has experience with the German Shepherd if possible. Together, perhaps you can pinpoint the cause of your dog's aggression and do something about it. An aggressive dog cannot be trusted, and a dog that cannot be trusted is not safe to have as a family pet. If the pet German Shepherd becomes untrustworthy, he cannot be kept in the home with the family. The family must get rid of the dog. In the worst case, the dog must be euthanised.

AGGRESSION TOWARD OTHER DOGS

A dog's aggressive behaviour toward another dog stems from not enough exposure to other dogs at an early age. If other dogs make your German Shepherd nervous and agitated, he will lash out as a protective mechanism. A dog who has not received

Dogs seem to act more aggressively on a short lead—be sure to keep your dog under control.

sufficient exposure to other canines tends to believe that he is the only dog on the planet. The animal becomes so dominant that he does not even show signs that he is fearful or threatened. Without growling or any other physical signal as a warning, he will lunge at and bite the other dog. A way to correct this is to let your German Shepherd approach another dog when walking on lead. Watch *very closely* and at the *very first* sign of aggression, correct your German Shepherd and pull him away. Scold him for any sign of discomfort, and then praise him when he ignores or tolerates the other dog. Keep this up until either he stops the aggressive behaviour, learns to ignore the other dog or even accepts other dogs. Praise him lavishly for his correct behaviour.

The German Shepherd is a high-energy dog that needs direction and structure. Here's a brilliant performance: Game Fair Scurry.

DOMINANT AGGRESSION
A social hierarchy is firmly established in a wild dog pack. The dog wants to dominate those under him and please those above him. Dogs know that there *must* be a leader. If you are not the obvious choice for

emperor, the dog will assume the throne! These conflicting innate desires are what a dog owner is up against when he sets about training a dog. In training a dog to obey commands, the owner is reinforcing that he is the top dog in the 'pack' and that the dog should, and should want to, serve his superior. Thus, the owner is suppressing the dog's urge to dominate by modifying his behaviour and making him obedient.

An important part of training is taking every opportunity to reinforce that you are the leader. The simple action of making your German Shepherd sit to wait for his food instead of allowing him to run up to get it when he wants it says that you control when he eats; he is dependent on you for food. Although it may be difficult, do not give in to your dog's wishes every time he whines at you or looks at you with pleading eyes. It is a constant effort to show the dog that his place in the pack is *at the bottom*. This is not meant to sound cruel or inhumane. You love your German Shepherd and you should

treat him with care and affection. You (hopefully) did not get a dog just so you could boss around another creature. Dog training is not about being cruel or feeling important, it is about moulding the dog's behaviour into what is acceptable and teaching him to live by your rules. In theory, it is quite simple: catch him in appropriate behaviour and reward him for it. Add a dog into the equation and it becomes a bit more try-

The establishment of the pecking order starts as soon as a few dogs get together. Obviously, the dog on its back is being submissive.

ceives himself at the top of the social heap, and will fight to defend his perceived status. The best way to prevent that is to never give him reason to think that he is in control in the first place. If you are having trouble training your German Shepherd and it seems as if he is constantly challenging your authority, seek the help of an obedience trainer or behavioural specialist. A professional will work with both you and your dog to teach you effective

Aggression is a very serious problem—an aggressive dog can be a dangerous dog.

DID YOU KNOW?

Fear in a grown dog is often the result of improper or incomplete socialisation as a pup, or it can be the result of a traumatic experience he suffered when young. Keep in mind that the term 'traumatic' is relative—something that you would not think twice about can leave a lasting negative impression on a puppy. If the dog experiences a similar experience later in life, he may try to fight back to protect himself. Again, this behaviour is very unpredictable, especially if you do not know what is triggering his fear.

ing, but as a rule of thumb, positive reinforcement is what works best.

With a dominant dog, punishment and negative reinforcement can have the opposite effect of what you are after. It can make a dog fearful and/or act out aggressively if he feels he is being challenged. Remember, a dominant dog per-

techniques to use at home. Beware of trainers who rely on excessively harsh methods; scolding is necessary now and then, but the focus in your training should always be on positive reinforcement.

If you can isolate what elicits the fear reaction, you can help the

Mounting is normally, but not always, a sexual behaviour.

SEXUAL BEHAVIOUR

Dogs exhibit certain sexual behaviours that may have influenced your choice of male or female when you first purchased your German Shepherd. Spaying/neutering will eliminate these behaviours, but if you are purchasing a dog that you wish to breed, you should be aware of what you will have to deal with throughout the dog's life.

Female dogs usually have two oestruses per year, each season lasting about three weeks. These are the only times in which a female dog will mate, and she usually will not allow this until the second week of the cycle. If a bitch is not bred during the heat cycle, it is not uncommon for her

dog get over it. Supervise your German Shepherd's interactions with people and other dogs, and praise the dog when it goes well. If he starts to act aggressively in a situation, correct him and remove him from the situation. Do not let people approach the dog and start petting him without your express permission. That way, you can have the dog sit to accept petting, and praise him when he behaves properly. You are focusing on praise and on modifying his behaviour by rewarding him when he acts appropriately. By being gentle and by supervising his interactions, you are showing him that there is no need to be afraid or defensive.

> **DID YOU KNOW?**
>
> Males, whether whole or altered, will mount most anything: a pillow, your leg or, much to your horror, even your neighbour's leg. As with other types of inappropriate behaviour, the dog must be corrected while in the act, which for once is not difficult. Often he will not let go! While a puppy, experimenting with his very first urges, his owners feel he needs to 'sow his oats' and allow the pup to mount. As the pup grows into a full-size dog, with full-size urges, it becomes a nuisance and an embarrassment. Males always appear as if they are trying to 'save the race,' more determined and strong than imaginable. While altering the dog at an appropriate age will limit the dog's desire, it usually does not remove it entirely.

massage their gums, to make their new teeth feel better and to exercise their jaws. This is a natural behaviour deeply imbedded in all things canine. Our role as owners is not to stop chewing, but to redirect it to positive, chew-worthy objects. Be an informed owner and purchase proper chew toys for your German Shepherd, like strong nylon bones made for large dogs. Be sure that the devices are safe

Is this a sly smile or isn't it?

to experience a false pregnancy, in which her mammary glands swell and she exhibits maternal tendencies toward toys or other objects.

Owners must further recognise that mounting is not merely a sexual expression but also one of dominance. Be consistent and persistent and you will find that you can 'move mounters.'

CHEWING

The national canine pastime is chewing! Every dog loves to sink his 'canines' into a tasty bone, but sometimes that bone is attached to his owner's hand! Dogs need to chew, to

and durable, since your dog's safety is at risk. Again, the owner is responsible for ensuring a dog-proof environment. The best answer is prevention: that is, put your shoes, handbags and other tasty objects in their proper places (out of the reach of the growing canine mouth). Direct puppies to their toys whenever you see them tasting the furniture legs or your pant leg. Make a loud noise to attract the pup's attention and immediately escort him to his chew toy and engage him with the toy for at

Dogs love to chew and they can be trained to retrieve if their favourite chew toy is used as the token to be fetched.

DID YOU KNOW?

Dogs and humans may be the only animals that laugh. They imitate the smile on their owner's face when they greet each other. The dog only smiles at its human friends. It never smiles at another dog or cat. Usually it rolls up its lips and shows its teeth in a clenched mouth while it rolls over onto its back begging for a soft scratch.

Jumping and climbing come naturally to a dog as athletic as the German Shepherd. Be certain your property is securely fenced or your dog may venture off on his own.

This dog could easily jump over the fence, but he has been trained not to. An easier alternative is to install a fence that is too high for the dog to get over.

products claim. Test out the product with your own dog before investing in a case of it.

JUMPING UP

Jumping up is a dog's friendly way of saying hello! Some dog owners do not mind when their dog jumps up, which is fine for them. The problem arises when guests come to the house and the dog greets them in the same manner—whether they like it or not! However friendly the greeting may be, chances are your visitors will not appreciate nearly being knocked over by 35 kgs of German Shepherd. The dog will not be able to distinguish upon whom he can jump and whom he cannot. Therefore, it is probably best to discourage this behaviour entirely.

Pick a command such as 'off' (avoid using 'down' since you will

least four minutes, praising and encouraging him all the while.

Some trainers recommend deterrents, such as hot pepper or another bitter spice or a product designed for this purpose, to discourage the dog from chewing on unwanted objects. This is sometimes reliable, though not as often as the manufacturers of such

DID YOU KNOW?

We all love our dogs and our dogs love us. They show their love and affection by licking us. This is not a very sanitary practice as dogs lick and sniff in some unsavory places. Kissing your dog on the mouth is strictly forbidden, as parasites can be transmitted in this manner.

A German Shepherd who gets regular exercise and play will be less likely to resort to destructive behaviour.

use that for the dog to lie down) and tell him 'off' when he jumps up. Place him on the ground on all fours and have him sit, praising him the whole time. Always lavish him with praise and petting when he is in the 'sit' position. That way you are still giving him a warm affectionate greeting, because you are as excited to see him as he is to see you!

DIGGING

Digging, which is seen as a destructive behaviour to humans, is actually quite a natural behaviour in dogs. Whether or not your dog is one of the 'earth dogs' (also known as terriers), his desire to dig can be irrepressible and most frustrating to his owners. When digging occurs in your garden, it is actually a normal behaviour redirected into something the dog can do in his everyday life. For example, in the wild a dog would be actively seeking food, making his own shelter, etc. He would be using his paws in a purposeful manner; he would be using them for his survival. Since you provide him with food and shelter, he has no need to use his paws for these purposes, and so the energy that he would be using manifests itself in the form of little holes all over your garden and flower beds.

Perhaps your dog is digging as a reaction to boredom—it is somewhat similar to someone eating a whole bag of crisps in front of the TV—because they are there and there is not anything better to do! Basically, the answer is to provide the dog with adequate play and exercise so that his mind and paws are occupied, and so that he feels as if he is doing something useful.

Of course, digging is easiest to control if it is stopped as soon as possible, but it is often hard to catch a

Dogs can't talk; they 'talk' by barking.

dog in the act, especially if he is alone in the garden during the day. If your dog is a compulsive digger and is not easily distracted by other activities, you can designate an area on your property where it is okay for him to dig. If you catch him digging in an off-limits area of the garden, immediately bring him to the approved area and praise him for digging there. Keep a close eye on him so that you can catch him, that is the only way he is going to understand what is permitted and what is not. If you bring him to a hole he dug an hour ago and tell him 'No,' he will understand that you are not fond of holes, or dirt, or flowers. If you catch him while he is stifle-deep in your tulips, that is when he will get your message.

If your dog won't look at you during training, don't try to force eye contact. This may be perceived as a sign of aggression and may provoke an attack.

BARKING
Dogs cannot talk—oh, what they would say if they could! Instead, barking is a dog's way of 'talking.' It can be somewhat frustrating because it is not always easy to tell what a dog means by his bark—is he excited, happy, frightened, angry? Whatever it is that the dog is trying to say, he should not be punished for barking. It is only when the barking becomes excessive, and when the excessive barking becomes a bad habit, does the behaviour need to be modified. If an intruder came into your home in the middle of the night and the dog barked a warning, wouldn't you be pleased? You would probably deem your dog a hero, a wonderful guardian and protector of the home. On the other hand, if a friend drops by unexpectedly and rings the doorbell and is greeted with a sudden sharp bark, you would probably be annoyed at the

dog. But isn't it just the same behaviour? The dog does not know any better…unless he sees who is at the door and it is someone he is familiar with, he will bark as a means of vocalising that his (and your) territory is being threatened. While your friend is not posing a threat, it is all the same to the dog. Barking is his means of letting you know that there is an intrusion, whether friend or foe, on your property. This type of barking is instinctive and should not be discouraged.

Excessive habitual barking, however, is a problem that should be corrected early on. As your German Shepherd grows up, you will be able to tell when his barking is purposeful and when it is for no reason. You will become able to distinguish your dog's different barks and with what they are associated. For example, the bark when someone comes to the door will be different from the bark when he is excited to see you. It is similar to a person's tone of voice, except that the dog has to rely totally on tone of voice because he does not have the benefit of using words. An incessant barker will be evident at an early age.

There are some things that encourage a dog to bark. For example, if your dog barks non-stop for a few minutes and you give him a treat to quiet him, he believes that you are rewarding him for barking. He will associate barking with getting a treat, and will keep doing it until he is rewarded.

FOOD STEALING

Is your dog devising ways of stealing food from your counter tops? If so, you must answer the following questions: Is your German Shepherd hungry, or is he 'constantly famished' like every other chow hound? Why is there food on the counter top? Face it, some dogs are more food-motivated than others; some dogs are totally obsessed by a slab of brisket and can only think of their next meal. Food

It is common that when one dog barks another will join in. You can imagine what a kennel full of German Shepherds must sound like.

DID YOU KNOW?

To encourage proper barking, you can teach your dog the command 'quiet.' When someone comes to the door and the dog barks a few times, praise him. Talk to him soothingly and when he stops barking, tell him 'quiet' and continue to praise him. In this sense you are letting him bark his warning, which is an instinctive behaviour, and then rewarding him for being quiet after a few barks. You may initially reward him with a treat after he has been quiet for a few minutes.

This German Shepherd looks like he's up to something!

stealing is terrific fun and always yields a great reward—FOOD, glorious food.

The owner's goal, therefore, is to make the 'reward' less rewarding, even startling! Plant a shaker can (an empty pop can with coins inside) on the counter so that it catches your pooch offguard. There are other devices available that will surprise the dog when he is looking for a mid-afternoon snack. Such remote-control devices, though not the first choice of some trainers, allow the correction to come from the object instead of the owner. These devices are also useful to keep the snacking hound from napping on furniture that is forbidden.

BEGGING

Just like food stealing, begging is a favourite pastime of hungry puppies! With that same reward—FOOD! Dogs quickly learn that their owners keep the 'good food' for themselves, and that we humans do not dine on kibble alone. Begging is a conditioned response related to a specific stimulus, time and place. The sounds of

the kitchen, cans and bottles opening, crinkling bags, the smell of food in preparation, etc., will excite the chow hound and soon the paws are in the air!

Here is the solution to stopping this behaviour: Never give into a beggar! You are rewarding the dog for sitting pretty, jumping up, whining and rubbing his nose into you by giving him that glorious reward—food. By ignoring the dog, you will (eventually) force the behaviour into extinction. Note that the behaviour likely

DID YOU KNOW?

When a dog bites there is always a good reason for it doing so. Many dogs are trained to protect a person, an area or an object. When that person, area or object is violated the dog will attack. A dog attacks with its mouth. It has no other means of attack. It never uses teeth for defense. It merely runs away or lays down on the ground when it is in an indefensible situation. Fighting dogs (and there are many breeds which fight) are taught to fight, but they also have a natural instinct to fight. This instinct is normally reserved for other dogs, though unfortunate accidents occur when babies crawl towards a fighting dog and the dog mistakes the crawling child as a potential attacker.

If a dog is a biter for no reason; if it bites the hand that feeds it; if it snaps at members of your family. See your veterinarian immediately for behavioural modification treatments.

gets worse before it disappears, so be sure there are not any 'softies' in the family who will give in to little 'Oliver' every time he whimpers, 'More, please.'

SEPARATION ANXIETY

Your German Shepherd may howl, whine or otherwise vocalise his displeasure at your leaving the house and his being left alone. This is a normal case of separation anxiety, but there are things that can be done to eliminate this problem. Your dog needs to learn that he will be fine on his own for a while and that he will not wither away if he is not attended to every minute of the day. In fact, constant attention can lead to separation anxiety in the first place. If you are endlessly coddling and cooing over your dog, he will come to expect this from you all of the time and it will be more traumatic for him when you are not there. Obviously, you enjoy spending time with your dog, and he thrives on your love and attention. However, it should not become a dependent relationship where he is heartbroken without you.

One thing you can do to minimise separation anxiety is to make your entrances and exits as low-key as possible. Do not give your dog a long drawn-out goodbye, and do not lavish him with hugs and kisses when you return. This is giving in to the attention that he craves, and it will only make him miss it more when you are away. Another thing you can try is to give your dog a treat when you leave; this will not only keep him occupied and keep his mind off the fact that you just left, but it will also help

PHOTO BY CHRISTINA URBAN.

An adult dog will often 'play fight' with a pup to let the pup know his place in the pack. The pup's not being hurt— in fact, adult dogs and pups usually make good companions for each other.

149

You should accustom your puppy to being left alone incrementally. However, he should be secure in his crate rather than loose in the home or garden.

him associate your leaving with a pleasant experience.

You may have to accustom your dog to being left alone in small increments, much like when you introduced your pup to his crate. Of course, when your dog starts whimpering as you approach the door, your first instinct will be to run to him and comfort him, but do not do it! Really—eventually he will adjust and be just fine if you take it in small steps. His anxiety stems from being placed in an unfamiliar situation; by familiarising him with being alone he will learn that he is okay. That is not to say you should purposely leave your dog home alone, but the dog needs to know that while he can depend on you for his care, you do not have to be by his side 24 hours a day.

When the dog is alone in the house, he should be confined to his crate or a designated dog-proof area of the house. This should be the area in which he sleeps, so he should already feel comfortable there and this should make him feel more at ease when he is alone. This

> **DID YOU KNOW?**
> Dogs get to know each other by sniffing each other's backsides.
>
> It seems that each dog has a telltale odor probably created by the anal glands. It also distinguishes sex and signals when a female will be receptive to a male's attention.
>
> Some dog's snap at the other dog's intrusion of their private parts.

is just one of the many examples in which a crate is an invaluable tool for you and your dog, and another reinforcement of why your dog should view his crate as a 'happy' place, a place of his own.

COPROPHAGIA

Faeces eating is, to most humans, one of the most disgusting behaviours that their dog could engage in, yet to the dog it is perfectly normal. It is hard for us to understand why a dog would want to eat its own faeces; he could be seeking certain nutrients that are missing from his diet, he could be just plain hungry, or he could be attracted by the pleasing (to a dog) scent. While coprophagia most often refers to the dog eating his own faeces, a dog may likely eat that of another animal as well if he comes across it. Vets have found that diets with a

Separation anxiety can be cured with time and patience.

low digestibility, containing relatively low levels of fibre and high levels of starch, increase coprophagia. Therefore, high-fibre diets may decrease the likelihood of dogs eating faeces. Both the consistency of the stool (how firm it feels in the dog's mouth) and the presence of undigested nutrients increase the

This troupe of police dogs would make any community feel well protected. These German Shepherds are employed by the Cheshire Police Force.

likelihood. Dogs often find the stool of cats and horses more palatable than that of other dogs. Once the dog develops diarrhoea from faeces eating, it will likely quit this distasteful habit, since dogs tend to prefer eating harder faeces.

To discourage this behaviour, first make sure that the food you are feeding your dog is nutritionally complete and that he is getting enough food. If changes in his diet do not seem to work, and no medical cause can be found, you will have to modify the behaviour through environmental control before it becomes a habit. There are some tricks you can try, such as adding an unpleasant-tasting substance to the faeces to make them unpalatable or adding

something to the dog's food which will make it unpleasant tasting after it passes through the dog. The best way to prevent your dog from eating his stool is to make it unavailable—clean up after he eliminates and remove any stool from the garden. If it is not there, he cannot eat it.

Never reprimand the dog for stool eating, as this rarely impresses the dog. Vets recommend distracting the dog while he is in the act of stool eating. Another option is to muzzle the dog when he is in the garden to relieve himself; this usually is effective within 30 to 60 days. Coprophagia most frequently is seen in pups 6 to 12 months of age, and usually disappears around the dog's first birthday.

Some animal behaviourists say that dogs begin stool eating to make it more difficult for predators to track them. It is not uncommon for nursing dams to eat their pups' excreta.

GLOSSARY

This glossary is intended to help you, the German Shepherd Dog owner, better understand the specific terms used in this book as well as other terms that might surface in discussions with your veterinary surgeon during his care of your German Shepherd Dog.

Abscess a pus-filled inflamed area of body tissue.

Acral lick granuloma unexplained licking of an area, usually the leg, that prevents healing of original wound.

Acute disease a disease whose onset is sudden and fast.

Albino an animal totally lacking in pigment (always white).

Allergy a known sensitivity that results from exposure to a given allergen.

Alopecia lack of hair.

Amaurosis an unexplained blindness from the retina.

Anaemia red-blood-cell deficiency.

Arthritis joint inflammation.

Atopic dermatitis congenital-allergen-caused inflammation of the skin.

Atrophy wasting away caused by faulty nutrition; a reduction in size.

Bloat gastric dilatation.

Calculi mineral 'stone' located in a vital organ, i.e., gall bladder.

Cancer a tumor that continues to expand and grow rapidly.

Carcinoma cancerous growth in the skin.

Cardiac arrhythmia irregular heartbeat.

Cardiomyopathy heart condition involving the septum and flow of blood.

Cartilage strong but pliable body tissue.

Cataract clouding of the eye lens.

Cherry eye third eyelid prolapsed gland.

Cleft palate improper growth of the two hard palates of the mouth.

Collie eye anomaly congenital defect of the back of the eye.

Congenital not the same as hereditary, but present at birth.

Congestive heart failure fluid buildup in lungs due to heart's inability to pump.

Conjunctivitis inflammation of the membrane that lines eyelids and eyeball.

Cow hocks poor rear legs that point inward; always incorrect.

Cryptorchid male animal with only one or both testicles undescended.

Cushing's disease condition caused by adrenal gland producing too much corticosteroid.

Cyst uninflamed swelling contain non-pus-like fluid.

Degeneration deterioration of tissue.

Demodectic mange red-mite infestation caused by *Demodex canis*.

Dermatitis skin inflammation.

Dew claw a functionless digit found on the inside of a dog's leg.

Diabetes insipidus disease of the hypothalamus gland resulting in animal passing great amounts of diluted urine.

Diabetes mellitus excess of glucose in blood stream.

Distemper contagious viral disease of dogs that can be most deadly.

Distichiasis double layer of eyelashes on an eyelid.

Dysplasia abnormal, poor development of a body part, especially a joint.

Dystrophy inherited degeneration.

Eclampsia potentially deadly disease in post-partum bitches due to calcium deficiency.

Ectropion outward turning of the eyelid; opposite of entropion.

Eczema inflammatory skin disease, marked by itching.

Edema fluid accumulation in a specific area.

Entropion inward turning of the eyelid.

Epilepsy chronic disease of the nervous system characterized by seizures.

Exocrine pancreatic insufficiency body's inability to produce enough enzymes to aid digestion.

False pregnancy pseudo-pregnancy, bitch shows all signs of pregnancy but there is no fertilization.

Follicular mange demodectic mange.

Gastric dilatation bloat caused by the dog's swallowing air resulting in distended, twisted stomach.

Gastroenteritis stomach or intestinal inflammation.

Gingivitis gum inflammation caused by plaque buildup.

Glaucoma increased eye pressure affecting vision.

Haematemesis vomiting blood.

Haematoma blood-filled swollen area.

Haematuria blood in urine.

Haemophilia bleeding disorder due to lack of clotting factor.

Haemorrhage bleeding.

Heat stroke condition due to over-heating of an animal.

Heritable an inherited condition.

Hot spot moist eczema characterised by dog's licking in same area.

Hyperglycemia excess glucose in blood.

Hypersensitivity allergy.

Hypertrophic cardiomyopathy left-ventricle septum becomes thickened and obstructs blood flow to heart.

Hypertrophic osteodystrophy condition affecting normal bone development.

Hypothyroidism disease caused by insufficient thyroid hormone.

Hypertrophy increased cell size resulting in enlargement of organ.

Hypoglycemia glucose deficiency in blood.

Idiopathic disease of unknown cause.

IgA deficiency immunoglobin deficiency resulting in digestive, breathing and skin problems.

Inbreeding mating two closely related animals, eg, mother—son.

Inflammation the changes that occur to a tissue after injury, characterised by swelling, redness, pain, etc.

Jaundice yellow colouration of mucous membranes.

Keratoconjunctivitis sicca dry eye.

Leukaemia malignant disease characterised by white blood cells released into blood stream.

Lick granuloma excessive licking of a wound, preventing proper healing.

Merle coat colour that is diluted.

Monorchid a male animal with only one testicle descended.

Neuritis nerve inflammation.

Nicitating membrane third eyelid pulling across the eye.

Nodular dermatofibrosis lumps on toes and legs, usually associated with cancer of kidney and uterus.

Osteochondritis bone or cartilage inflammation.

Outcrossing mating two breed representatives from different families.

Pancreatitis pancreas inflammation.

Pannus chronic superficial keratitis, affecting pigment and blood vessels of cornea.

Panosteitis inflammation of leg bones, characterised by lameness.

Papilloma wart.

Patellar luxation slipped kneecap, common in small dogs.

Patent ductus arteriosus an open blood vessel between pulmonary artery and aorta.

Penetrance frequency in which a trait shows up in offspring of animals carrying that inheritable trait.

Periodontitis acute or chronic inflammation of tissue surround the tooth.

Pneumonia lung inflammation.

Progressive retinal atrophy congenital disease of retina causing blindness.

Pruritis persistent itching.

Retinal atrophy thin retina.

Seborrhea dry scurf or excess oil deposits on the skin.

Stomatitis mouth inflammation.

Tumor solid or fluid-filled swelling resulting from abnormal growth.

Uremia waste product buildup in blood due to disease of kidneys.

Uveitis inflammation of the iris.

Von Willebrand's disease hereditary bleeding disease.

Wall eye lack of colour in the iris.

Weaning separating the mother from her dependent, nursing young.

Zoonosis animal disease communicable to humans.

INDEX

Page numbers in boldface indicate illustrations.

Acquisition, 34
Acral lick disease, 111, **111**
Acrodermatitis, 100
Adult diets, 54
Age, 120
Aggression, 138
—dominant, 140
—toward other dogs, 139
Agility, 19
Agility trials, 88, 133
Airplanes, 63
Allergies
—airborne, 101
—food, 101
Alsatian Wolf Dog, 12
American Kennel Club, 135
Anaemia, 114, 116
Ancylostoma caninum, 113, **114**
Ascaris lumbricoides, 113, **113**
Auto-immune skin conditions, 110
Automobiles, 62
Axelrod, Dr. Herbert R., 112
Backpacking, 87
Barking, 146
Bathing, 17, 59
Begging, 148
Behaviour, 137–152
Blankets, 39
Boarding, 64
Bone diseases, 22
Bowls, 42
Breed standard, 26, 125
Breeder, 34
Brown dog tick, **109**
Brushing, 57
Burial, 122
Canadian Kennel Club, 135
Canine cough, 95
Cat flea, **104**, 106
Cataracts, 22
Cemetery, 122
Challenge Certificates, 126
Champion, 126, 132
Championship Shows, 126
Characteristics, 15
—personality, 17
—physical, 15
Chewing, 50, 74, 143
Cheyletiella, 110
Chiggers, 110
Cleaning supplies, 42
Clinical signs, 91
Coat, 16
Collar, 42, 79
Collie eye, 22
Come, 83
Commands, 81–86

Commitment, 35
Control, 74
Coprophagia, 151
Crate, 38
—travel, 62, 63
Crate training, 73, 77
Crufts Dog Show, 125
Crying, 51
Ctenocephalides canis, 104, **104**, 106, **106**
Ctenocephalides felis, **104**, 106
De-fleaing the home, 107
Demodex, 110
Dermacentor variabilis, **108**, 109, **109**
Development schedule, 71
Diet, 53
—adult, 54
—puppy, 54
—senior, 55
Digging, 145
Dirofilaria immitis, **116**, **117**
Discipline, 77
Distemper, 94
Dog flea, 104, **104**, 106, **106**
—eggs, **104**
Down, 81
Down/stay, 83
Dry bath, 60
Ear cleaning, 60
Ear mites, 60, 110
Echinococcus multilocularis, 115
Elbow dysplasia, **22,** 23
Epilepsy, 22
Euthanasia, 121
Exemption shows, 127
Exercise, 57
Eye diseases, 22
Family introductions, 46
Federation Cynologique Internationale, 133, 135
Feeding, 53
Field trials, 132
Fleas, 102–109
—life cycle, 104, **105**
Food intolerance, 101
Food problems, 102
Food rewards, 79, 81, 82, 83, 84, 86
Food stealing, 147
German Shepherd Dog Club of America, 13
Grooming, 17, 57
Guarding livestock, 9
Heart problems, 22
Heartworms, 92, 115, **116**, **117**
Heat cycle, 142
Heel, 84
Hektor von Linksrhein, 10, 11
Hemophilia A, 22
Hepatitis, 94
Herding, 19, 20
Hereditary conditions, 21
Hip dysplasia, 13, 21, 96, 98, 99, **99**
History, 9–13

Hookworms, 113, 114, **114, 115**
Horand von Grafath, 11
Housebreaking, 70–77
Housing, 72
Hypertrophic osteodystrophy, 22
Identification, 64, 65, 96
Inbreeding, 11
International Beauty Champion, 133
International Champion, 133
International Trial Champion, 133
Ivermectin, 107, 114
Ixode dog tick, **109**
Jumping up, 144
Kennel Club, The, 126, 135
Lead, 41, 79
Lice, **107**
Life span, 23, 119–121
Limited shows, 127
Linebreeding, 11
Lost dogs, 64
Lyme disease, 109
Mange, 110
Match shows, 127
Mites, 110, **110, 111**
Mosquitoes, 116
Myasthenia gravis, 22
Nail clipping, 61
Neutering, 96
Nipping, 50
Obedience classes, 86
Obedience trials, 86
Obesity, 55
Oestrus, 142
OK, 85
Open Shows, 126
Osteochondritis dissecans, 22
Overbreeding, 12
Owner considerations, 33
Owner suitability, 18
Pannus, 22
Panosteitis, 22
Parainfluenza, 94
Parasites
—bites, 100
—external, 102
—internal, 111
Parvovirus, 95
Patent ductus arteriosis, 22
Persistent right aortic arch, 22
Phylax Society, 10
Poisonous plants, 45
Police work, 11, 20
Preventative medicine, 92
Primary shows, 127
Psoroptes bovis, **110**
Punishment, 77, 141
Puppies
—diets, 54
—problems, 48
—purchasing, 34

Puppy-proofing, 43
Radiograph, 91
Register of Merit, 13
Retinal dysplasia, 22
Rewards, 79
Rhabditis, **114**
Rhipicephalus sanguineus, **109**
Rocky Mountain spotted fever, 109
Roundworms, 112, **112, 113, 114**
Scabies, 110
Schedule, 74
Schutzhund, 20, 88
Seeing Eye® Foundation, 32
Senior diets, 55
Senior dogs, 119–121
Separation anxiety, 149
Sex, 35
Sexual behaviour, 142
Show Champion, 132
Sit, 81
Sit/stay, 82
Skin problems, 97
—auto-immune, 110
—inherited, 98
Socialisation, 48
Standard, 26, 125
Stay, 82
Stool eating, 151
S.V., 11, 13
Symptoms, 91
Tapeworms, 114, **115**
Tattoo, 96
Thorndike, Dr. Edward, 78
Thorndike's Theory of Learning, 78
Ticks, **108,** 109, **109,** 110
Toxocara canis, 112
Toys, 40
Tracheobronchitis, 95
Training, 63
—commands, 81–86
—consistency, 49
—equipment, 79
Travelling, 62
Treats, 79
Vaccinations, 94
—schedule, 95
Verein fuer Deutsche Schaeferhunde, 11, 135
Versatility, 19
Veterinary surgeon, 44, 91
Von Stephanitz, Max Emil Friedrich, 10, 11
Von Willebrand's, 22
Walking, 85
Water, 55
Whining, 51
Working tests, 132
Working trials, 129
World Dog Show, 135
World Wars, 12
X-ray, 91

My German Shepherd

PUT YOUR PUPPY'S FIRST PICTURE HERE

Dog's Name _____

Date _____ Photographer _____